No

Will

Set

You

Free

OTHER WORKS BY
MICHAEL J. TOUGIAS

Rescue of the Bounty: A True Story of Disaster and Survival in Superstorm Sandy, Simon & Schuster, coauthor Douglas Campbell

A Storm Too Soon: A True Story of Disaster, Survival, and an Incredible Rescue, Simon & Schuster

Overboard! A True Blue-Water Odyssey of Disaster and Survival, Simon & Schuster

Fatal Forecast: An Incredible True Story of Disaster and Survival at Sea, Simon & Schuster

Ten Hours Until Dawn: The True Story of Heroism and Tragedy Aboard the Can Do, St. Martin's Press, American Library Association Best Book of the Year Selection

The Finest Hours: The True Story of the US Coast Guard's Most Daring Sea Rescue, Simon & Schuster, coauthor Casey Sherman, finalist for the Massachusetts Book Award

The Waters Between Us: A Boy, A Father, Outdoor Misadventures, and the Healing Power of Nature

Until I Have No Country: A Novel of King Philip's Indian War, Christopher Matthews Publishing

King Philip's War: The History and Legacy of America's Forgotten Conflict, WW Norton, coauthor Eric Schultz

Above & Beyond: John F. Kennedy and America's Most Dangerous Spy Mission, PublicAffairs, coauthor Casey Sherman

There's a Porcupine in My Outhouse: Misadventures of a Mountain Man Wannabe, On Cape Publications, winner of the Independent Publishers Association Best Nature Book of the Year Award

So Close to Home: A True Story of an American Family's Fight for Survival During WWII, Pegasus Books, coauthor Alison O'Leary

River Days: Exploring the Connecticut River from Source to Sea, On Cape Publications

AMC's Best Day Hikes Near Boston, Appalachian Mountain Club

Nature Walks in Central and Western MA

Exploring the Hidden Charles

Country Roads of Massachusetts

Quiet Places of Massachusetts

New England Wild Places

The Cringe Chronicles (with Kristin Tougias)

Middle Reader Books: *The Finest Hours, A Storm Too Soon, Attacked At Sea, Into the Blizzard, Abandon Ship, Claws, and Ghost of the Forest*

Quabbin: A History and Explorers Guide

The Blizzard of '78

Extreme Survival (Winter 2023)

NO
Will Set
You
Free

Quit Overthinking and
Say Yes to Self-Happiness

MICHAEL J. TOUGIAS

NYT bestselling author

CORAL GABLES

Cover Design & Art Direction: Morgane Leoni
Layout & Design: Katia Mena

For permission requests, please contact the publisher at:
Mango Publishing Group
2850 S Douglas Road, 4th Floor
Coral Gables, FL 33134 USA
info@mango.bz

For special orders, quantity sales, course adoptions and corporate sales, please email the publisher at sales@mango.bz. For trade and wholesale sales, please contact Ingram Publisher Services at customer.service@ingramcontent.com or +1.800.509.4887.

No Will Set You Free: Quit Overthinking and Say Yes to Self-Happiness

Library of Congress Cataloging-in-Publication number: 2021953171
ISBN: (print) 978-1-68481-604-0, (ebook) 978-1-64250-835-2
BISAC category code SEL023000, SELF-HELP / Personal Growth / Self-Esteem

Printed in the United States of America

TABLE OF CONTENTS

AUTHOR'S NOTE

I usually devour books, often reading them in two or three days. However, with *No Will Set You Free*, you might want to consider reading a chapter or two each day, preferably in the morning, and then implementing some of the techniques and mindsets while they are fresh in your memory. And after you have read the first three or four chapters, the book is written so you can jump ahead and read a particular chapter that speaks directly to your current situation. Then you can go back and pick up where you left off. The cumulative effect of each chapter topic gives reinforcement to your quest to take back your time.

By the time you reach the end of the book, a couple of weeks or more will have gone by, and you should see the blossoming of real change in your life. And that is just the beginning. As you get better at reclaiming your time, it's my hope that you are on the permanent path of less stress, fewer commitments, and more joy.

BREAK THOSE CHAINS!

We have all been taught to seize the moment and say yes to opportunities, invitations, and requests on our time. Most of us say yes without thinking. Society has trained us to be polite and accommodate a friend, take that promotion, go to that party. We have said yes for so long we don't even consider its downside.

Studies have shown that we underestimate how difficult it is to say no. Some of that research is sprinkled into the following pages. Researcher and Professor Vanessa Bohns, PhD at Cornell University, has performed studies where participants asked more than 14,000 strangers various requests. The strangers complied at a rate far higher than the requesters predicted. Compliance wasn't necessarily because the strangers wanted to perform the task, but rather their dread of saying no. "Many people," writes Dr. Bohns, "agree to do things—even things they would prefer not to do—simply to avoid the considerable discomfort of saying no." You might be one of those people.

This little book will break you of that habit. It will make you reconsider how you conduct yourself in your job and how you use your free time. I know this because I was a yes man. But through a long journey, I learned the power of *No*. I'm going to share that journey, and hopefully, some of my earlier predicaments and faulty decision-making will resonate with you, and you'll say, *I've done the exact same thing.*

By learning the strength and freedom within one simple word, *No*, I turned what I considered an average life into an extraordinary one. In the pages that follow, you will see how I transitioned out of a soul-sucking job and launched a career that I was passionate about—one that brought me joy and more wealth than I had dreamed of. That was just beginning. Once I learned that *No* could set me free, my life took off in various new directions—all of them more fulfilling than where I had been. Some of those stories are in this book to show you that you too can harness *No* and start on a path of continued happiness.

I'll wager many of those reading this don't fully realize what a yes person you are. But because you picked up this book, you have an inkling that you need to make some changes in your life to better serve the real you. We only have one life, and the most important aspect in our control is time: how, where, and with whom we portion it out. The trick is to use it the way you *really* want to and not get swept up by spending it the way others would have you handle it.

This does not mean you are going to be selfish. On the contrary, you're going to have more time to help others.

Finally, what is the most common complaint that we hear, both from friends, family, and ourselves? It is probably "I'm stressed." The power of *No* will relieve that stress and lead you to a calmer, unhurried, and even more productive life.

So come with me on this voyage and learn how to navigate the churning seas of "yes" and find smoother sailing with *no*.

WHY WE SAY YES
(AND WHY NO SEEMS SO HARD)

I was afraid it would hurt his feelings...I didn't want to be impolite. Society has brainwashed us at a young age to be "pleasers."

A friend has called you and made an incredible offer. He or she has two free tickets for excellent seats at an upcoming game of a professional sports team that he knows you love. For me, that call was for an important Patriots home game, just a half hour from my house. This friend, whom I'll call Bob, was a relatively new acquaintance, someone whose company I always enjoyed whenever we got together.

Most football fans would have jumped at the chance and said, "Wow, thank you!" But that is not what I *felt*. I wasn't pumped up to go, but I didn't want to let my buddy down, so I stalled for time and said something like, "That is really nice of you. Let me check with my girlfriend and make sure she doesn't have something planned that day, and I'll get back to you."

Now you might say, that is the coward's way out, and maybe it was. But I needed a little time to think about why I wasn't enthusiastic about going. The answers came within a couple of minutes. The playoff contest would be played outside in December, I'd been to a game before and found watching on TV was just as rewarding, and finally, it would be a several-hour commitment—traffic, waiting in line, etc.

But the biggest reason going to the game didn't interest me was that I was looking forward to a quiet Sunday to work on a writing project. Simply put, the prospect of writing and the accompanying feeling of productivity toward a personal goal was more important to me than the Patriots.

So why couldn't I tell my friend that? I was afraid it would hurt his feelings; after all, he went out of his way to make a generous offer to me. I didn't want to be impolite.

Now, had this offer come to me many years ago, I would have ignored my true feeling about the game and accepted the offer. I'm sure I would have enjoyed the contest and his companionship, but in the back of my mind—while waiting in traffic to get to the stadium—I would likely have been thinking, *Why did I accept? I could have been working on my project and watched the last quarter of the game on TV.*

Instead, I called up my friend and said, "I'm going to pass on the Patriots. I'm just not into live events with crowds, and the cold weather gets to me. I also have a writing project I need to work on. I sure appreciate you thinking of me. Let's watch another game at my house sometime soon."

I made sure Bob knew I wasn't wild about crowds because I didn't want him to ask me another time and feel uncomfortable all over again. (Too often, after a person says no, they feel a bit guilty, and the next time an invite comes, they feel a self-induced pressure compelling them to say yes.) And I closed my conversation with the intention that I would still like to watch games with my friend if they were on TV. That way, he knew my response had nothing to do with our friendship but just my personal preference for watching football. (And writers work unusual days and hours.)

Did my friend sound disappointed? I didn't think so; he did what any good friend would do and respected my decision. Not everyone would act that way, but if so, are they really friends?

My answer to Bob was not a couple of minutes in the making, but years of transitioning from an automatic "yes man" to a "let me think about it" man.

Notice that I didn't give Bob an honest answer right off the bat but instead said I'd get back to him. I use this example because it shows that even now, after years of saying no, it's not always an easy thing to do. But I don't beat myself up when I occasionally make up an excuse rather than explain the real reason for a no. After all, during my entire childhood, it was ingrained in me to be polite and put the other person's feelings first. And throughout my twenties and into my thirties, societal norms and peer pressure only reinforced that notion. It wasn't until an event occurred in my mid-thirties that I started consciously trying to break myself of my "yes habit." (I'll explain more about how that event helped free me in a later chapter.)

I learned that saying no is not being impolite but rather a way to be a more thoughtful and conscious person regarding *how you spend your time.* Time is the most important thing you have, and yet we give it away without consideration. In this book you will see that taking back control of your time can be done, and it is not selfish or discourteous.

Had my friend Bob called me with a different request, saying, "Do you want to go to the Patriots game? My wife and I are talking about a divorce, and I need to get out of the house," my response would have been, "Of course." It would be clear to me that he *needed* company.

But what if those calls kept coming, and Bob asked me to join him every weekend? My response would be different once again. I would have realized that even though we had gotten together three or four times in a row and discussed his marital situation, he needed more than I could offer. I would have explained that I was busy and, later in the conversation, suggest how beneficial talking to a therapist would be for him as he navigated the marital issues.

At some point, you have done your best, and continuing to say yes—giving your time to another—is unproductive and draining. You will know when to say no (gently). I can see many readers rolling their eyes, thinking, *Easy for you to say; you don't know my situation and how these people depend on me. I can't just say no.*

Why is saying no so hard? Why do we cave in to so many requests for our time? It's because we feel uneasy turning down a request, and rather than be uncomfortable for a minute or two, we say yes and then later kick ourselves. That is perfectly natural because society has brainwashed us at a young age to be "pleasers." We want to be helpful. We want to be connected. We don't want hurt feelings. Some of us have such a strong need to be wanted, we blindly agree to every request. But if you keep doing that, soon you are living someone else's idea for your life, and not your own. You make others' agendas complete and leave yours unfulfilled.

My mother was the politest person on the planet, and through observational osmosis, I'm sure that rubbed off me, making it difficult to say no to people. Your experience may be that you were raised by "pleasers" or people with such big hearts that they wanted to help everyone. No matter what the reason, you are far from alone in your avoidance of saying no. And don't let anyone fool you that transitioning from a "yes person" to a "let me think about it person" is easy. I feel I've made that important change in my life—but I still slip up!

Recently I was introduced to a fellow fisherman from out of state who had just moved to my neighborhood. He called me up and suggested we go fishing. Now, I'm a fishing fanatic, so that was an easy "yes" for me. But my error occurred when he said he explored a particular beach, and it looked like a great striped bass spot for early morning. He was excited and enthusiastic and described the beach in detail. I knew that beach quite well and never had much fishing luck there over the years. But wanting to be accommodating, I said sure— even though I had just been to a different nearby beach that had fish blitzing it each morning for the past two days.

You know where this story is going. I should have said no to his beach and directed him to the better one. We went to the beach he recommended and caught nothing, while another friend reported to me that "my" beach still held fish.

Think about it—by trying to be polite, I let someone brand new to the area pick the spot to fish when I knew a much better place.

It can be damn tough to say no. But I'm going to share some secrets that make it easier to say no and offer different ways to say no without using those words. Once you are an old pro at determining how to use your time, "no" will come easy to you. But we all have to start somewhere.

TRY IT:

- For the next two weeks, be hyper-aware when others request a portion of your time. Be cognizant of those instances when you say "yes" even though your gut tells you no. You may not feel comfortable saying no to some situations at this particular time, but know that with the help of this book and your determination, *you* will soon be deciding where your energies should be directed and not someone else.

- Repeat after me: "I'm not going to make another person's agenda complete and leave mine unfulfilled." Type this quote up and post it where you will see it every morning.

- As a rule, start incorporating this mantra into your decisions: Do I feel a bit of excitement about the request? If the answer is negative, it's your first indication you should probably say no.

WRITE THE ONE TAKE-AWAY FROM THIS CHAPTER THAT WILL GIVE YOU THE MOST BENEFIT AND YOU WILL WORK ON DAILY.

_____

_____

_____

_____

_____

_____

_____

_____

_____

_____

_____

_____

_____

_____

_____

_____

_____

_____

_____

_____

_____

_____

NO TO GROUP PRESSURE— AT ANY AGE!

They were putting the full court press on me. But it didn't hurt that at age sixty-five I had about thirty-five years of practice of not letting someone else's agenda dictate how I would respond.

The term "peer pressure" conjures up images of young adults succumbing to coercion from others of a similar age. However, that pressure is felt at any age, and it's my mission to illustrate how to stand your ground when you feel comfortable with your convictions.

Here is a recent situation that I found myself in that I hope serves to keep you steadfast even when you are the lone dissenting voice. I had been hired to speak at a corporate outing and the organizer and I agreed to an outdoor setting. This occurred in the middle of the COVID-19 pandemic, and although small groups were allowed to gather indoors, I wasn't going to take any chances. The organizer originally wanted me to speak indoors, but I declined, saying I was only doing outdoor events with proper social distancing. They decided to accommodate me and have the event in an open-air tent set up behind a restaurant.

When I arrived to give my presentation, the organizer greeted me by the tent and told me there had been a change of plans. The event would be held inside because senior management felt it was too cold outside for both themselves and their special guests, who were their top clients. The organizer laid this out not as a request but as if it were a done deal, and she said everyone was already in the function room.

This was awkward, and I made it more so by saying, "You will have to have your meeting without me. We agreed that I would speak outside. When we talked on the phone, I explained I was not doing indoor events because of COVID."

The organizer, a senior vice president of the company, looked stunned. She was not used to having someone say no to her. When she found her voice, she said, "Let's go inside, and you will see that it is perfectly safe."

"No, thank you," I said. I told her no hard feelings—they only had to reimburse me for travel, and they could keep the speaking fee. Then I said goodbye.

NO WILL SET YOU FREE

Again, she looked stunned but quickly recovered. "Okay. Why don't you wait right here while I talk to the president?" I agreed. Five minutes later, the president and a couple of other senior managers came out and said, "We understand your concern, but at least come inside and take a look at the setting. I think that will make you comfortable and eliminate any fears you have."

They were putting the full-court press on me. My reaction surprised me. Instead of feeling nervous, I felt calm. I was comfortable with my decision. Saying no to that group felt natural; there was nothing they could say to make me change my mind. I have always put my health first, and I wasn't going to change that now. My comfort level may have come from believing in the power of no, even when you are outnumbered, and it didn't hurt that at age sixty-five, I had about thirty-five years of practice of not letting someone else's agenda dictate how I would respond.

Will I ever get hired by that company in the future? Probably not. But as I left the group, I felt a feeling of peace and contentment. I can only imagine how ill at ease I would have been if I let them pressure me to do something contrary to my core values. Money, power, and group pressure cannot buy a "yes" answer when you follow your inner compass and not theirs.

TRY IT:

- Time is the most important thing you have, and yet we give it away without consideration. From this day forward, vow to be thoughtful of how you decide to spend your time. Later in the book, you'll learn a variety of ways to say no right off the bat, but for now, do the following: any time someone asks for a chunk of your time, and you don't feel enthusiastic about complying, say, "I'll get back to you." If you are too uncomfortable to call the person and say no, do it in an email or a text and simply say, "I can't do it." If you want to give a reason, say, "I have another commitment" or "Too much on my plate right now."

- Promise yourself that when it comes to your inner convictions, you will not do something that violates them because of pressure from others. When you feel your health might be jeopardized, stick to your guns.

NO AND YOU

What prompts you to say "yes" to almost everything?

- feeling too uncomfortable to say no
- fear of missing out
- subconscious impulse
- seeking distraction from a challenging task
- garnering favor—"yes man"
- lessons ingrained from stressed-out parents/spouses/siblings
- worrying about hurting the requestor's feelings
- thinking *these people depend on me, and only I can get the job done*

These are just some of the reasons why you might be saying "yes" much too often. Knowing your reason for saying yes is the first step in overcoming this obstacle and being comfortable with "no."

WRITE THE ONE TAKE-AWAY FROM THIS CHAPTER THAT WILL GIVE YOU THE MOST BENEFIT AND YOU WILL WORK ON DAILY.

_____

_____

_____

_____

_____

_____

_____

_____

_____

_____

_____

_____

_____

_____

_____

_____

_____

_____

_____

_____

THE DAY I LEARNED
THE BEAUTY OF NO

ZEROING IN ON AN IMPORTANT PROJECT
OR YOUR SPECIAL PURPOSE

*Saying no is so much easier if you
have a particular goal, a mission
that you want to devote free time to.
Ask yourself, what would I want to
do if I only had more free time?*

When I was in my early thirties, I knew I wanted to be an author. But I had children, a mortgage, and a secure job as a manager in the insurance industry. I couldn't just quit my job and begin writing, hoping that the money would follow. I worked long hours in my management position and devoted much of the weekends to spending time with my family. So how was I to become an author and still be a father, husband, and manager? The answer was to say no to almost everything else other than the day job and family. It would be difficult, but I thought the payoff would be worth the sacrifice.

I'd been writing articles for magazines and newspapers, and I had a clear idea of the time commitment that would go into writing a book. I estimated that it would take me at least a year of "moonlighting" to complete the first few chapters of the book I had in mind. And beyond the typical moonlighting—where I worked bleary-eyed on the project well into the night after the kids had gone to bed—I'd need to carve out other time. I made an internal vow that I'd say yes to time with my wife, kids, corporate job, and exercise, and no to most everything else for one year and see if I had enough research and writing done to land a book contract. And so, I began saying no to restaurant dinners, no to most parties unless my wife really wanted to go, no to weekend trips fishing or golfing with buddies, no to reading the newspaper, no to television, etc.

What I did is certainly not for everybody, and you do need understanding from your partner if you have one. But if you have a shot at a dream and all that is needed is extra time, try an experiment like mine temporarily.

I used bits of time in some unlikely places to help me on my journey. On the train ride into Boston, I stopped reading and instead wrote rough drafts of my work; on lunch breaks, I left the group I hung out with (who mostly bitched about their jobs or talked sports) and I ran to the Boston Public Library for research material. A few minutes here, a few there, and

I was moving the ball forward. Somedays, my work/family obligations took up most of the day, but I told myself to do one thing, no matter how small, to help "the project."

I never considered myself a TV watcher, but I usually viewed an hour of television after the kids went to bed. Giving up that one hour a day over a year bought me another big block of time. I also said no to alcohol. Before the writing project/experiment, I was in the habit of having two glasses of wine around 7:00 p.m.—my reward for surviving another day in the business world. I quickly found that those glasses of wine took part of my focus away, and clear, concise writing was next to impossible. Whenever I reached for the wine bottle, I told myself, *no, your reward will come when you are holding your book in your hand.*

While I wouldn't want to spend my whole life with this single-minded mission approach, in the end, I found the trade-off well worth it. Sure, I missed some fun, rest, and relaxation, but I did land that book contract. That was the day I realized the full potential of saying no. That contract launched me on a career that I had only previously dreamed about and set in motion my efforts to try other paths that once seemed impossible.

Saying no is so much easier if you have a particular goal or mission that you want to devote free time to. Ask yourself, *what would I want to accomplish or change if I only had more free time?* You might identify three or four objectives, then choose one to try first. Make that extra time needed by the power of no. Before you make a single commitment or social engagement, make sure it passes the test of the all-important question: "Will this bring me joy?" If the answer is negative, let it go and devote that time to the objective you have identified as incredibly important. It will require hard work but may bring lasting happiness.

Once you realize that every time you say yes to anything other than your special project your time is being diverted from the mission. We all have the same finite time in a day, and it's up to you to say no to several daily habits. That will allow you to give a big yes to your special project. When you say no to the many requests and invitations that don't excite you, you are saying yes to a handful of core activities that are important to you.

Creating a special "Room of No" is yet another way to help you achieve your project. You're going to need a big block of uninterrupted time to pursue that goal of learning to play the guitar, analyzing stocks, researching new occupations, or painting that masterpiece. In the Room of No, text messages, phone calls, and emails are not allowed. This is your time, so make the most of it without disruptions so you can focus and make big strides toward your desired outcome. In that room and in that time, all your thoughts and efforts are devoted to your special project, and you will say no to anything unrelated.

The key is to have a purpose. Then anything unrelated to that purpose becomes noise. And if you have your "Room of No" or your "Two hours of No," the noise gets blocked out, or better yet, the distractions can't reach you. At first, you might think, *I'm missing out*, but once you get started on your goal and gain some traction, the missing-out feeling evaporates under the satisfaction of the strides you are making. If you say yes to every offer and distraction, your time is frittered away, and you miss out on what's important to you.

In the book *Tuesdays with Morrie*, Lou Gehrig's disease slowly takes Morrie's energy and life force. But Morrie has no regrets about the life he has lived. One of his secrets is in a simple statement he made about how too many people "were chasing the wrong things.... Devote yourself to creating something that gives you purpose and meaning."

TRY IT:

- Identify one or two areas of your life you want to improve. Make the time to achieve your goal by saying no to almost everything other than your family, your current job if you are working, and your health. Understand that for big goals, you have to make sacrifices, but keep your eyes on the prize and be the master of how you spend your time. A remarkable outcome might be just around the corner!

- If you have long harbored accomplishing a difficult goal or completing an important project but never had the time to get started, there is one simple way to carve out the hours needed. Before you make any other commitments, ask yourself *will this bring me or someone I love joy?* You will find many engagements don't meet that test. It will be easier to say no because you will use that saved time for your endeavor.

NO AND YOU

Is there too much "yes" in your life?

- Are you stressed from being overscheduled?
- Are your closest friends and family members expressing feelings of neglect?
- Are you getting enough sleep and
  "me" time?
- Are you able to enjoy your favorite pas-
  times without watching the clock?
- Do you often leave tasks unfinished or
  often need last-minute help?
- Is there one important project you
  have wanted to do for years but never
  found the time?

WRITE THE ONE TAKE-AWAY FROM THIS CHAPTER THAT WILL GIVE YOU THE MOST BENEFIT AND YOU WILL WORK ON DAILY.

_____

_____

_____

_____

_____

_____

_____

_____

_____

_____

_____

_____

_____

_____

_____

_____

_____

_____

_____

_____

_____

_____

WHEN TO LEAN TOWARD YES (AND SAY NO TO NAGGING PROBLEMS)

In many cases, friends and family members say no because they are resistant to change, even change that might benefit them.

Many of the "no" examples in this book involve requests for your time that you don't feel enthusiastic about. But when it comes to ideas, advice, and new ways of looking at challenges, you don't want to shut out opportunity by saying no without thoughtful consideration. You probably have friends or family members who verbalize a problem, and because you care about them, you offer solutions or a different perspective. As you share your ideas, the person with the issue interrupts and says, "No, that's not me." And you haven't even completed your suggestions!

In many cases, these friends and family members say no because they are resistant to change, even change that might benefit them. They have closed their mind to your counsel.

It's almost as if they don't want to solve the problem they originally shared with you.

At the least, we should all keep an open mind to helpful ideas shared by others. We should seriously deliberate the advice, the new idea, and the different outlook. Some suggestions will be discarded, but others that hold promise should be given half a chance. Don't become one of those people who never solves a problem because the solution is outside their comfort zone. Some people like to wallow in their misery and bring up the same issue repeatedly without taking a single step to solving the problem. For them, the quick "no" response is a knee-jerk reaction showing their unwillingness to do the work to improve their lives.

Maybe you fall into this group? If so, here's the outlook you want to take: Say no to living with this ongoing problem but say yes to a solution that seems like it might help—no matter how uncomfortable it might be for you. Remember, you want to achieve your fullest potential, the real you, and be set free. You can't do that if you recognize a nagging dilemma but have dodged trying to solve it. To eradicate the problem, you must be brutally honest with yourself and ask, "Am I complaining about an issue without fully considering all the helpful advice given to me?" If you fall into this category, you are saying "yes" to the problem but "no" to the potential solutions!

TRY IT:

- Ask yourself if there are one or two nagging troubles in your personal life that only you can resolve. To truly be set free, a conscious effort must be made to say no to lingering issues that hold you back and say yes to experimenting with various solutions. The ultimate answer or key may be painful in the short run but could open up opportunities you never even dreamed of in the long run.

- If a friend or family member has a problem they always complain about, your next conversation might include a gentle no. You might say, "Let's not keep revisiting this issue until you have tried some of the solutions I've offered."

- Be open to new experiences. I'd rather say no to something I've already done that did not bring me joy, thereby saving my yeses to act upon a new opportunity or experience I've never tried.

- Most of the regrets people have when looking back at their lives are for new experiences that they *didn't do*. Multiple studies bear this out, including Cornell University's Thomas Gilovich's findings that one of the biggest regrets is not being open enough or brave enough to take advantage of an important opportunity. Another interesting source is Bronnie Ware's research and book *The Top Five Regrets of the Dying*. The first two regrets tie into the messages in this book not doing what others pressure you toward and learning to set boundaries at work. Regret #1 is not having "the courage to be true to myself and not the life others expected of me." Regret #2 is "I wish I hadn't worked so hard." My goal in this book is for all of us to avoid those two regrets by learning when to say no so that we have time and space for the important yeses!

WRITE THE ONE TAKE-AWAY FROM THIS CHAPTER THAT WILL GIVE YOU THE MOST BENEFIT AND YOU WILL WORK ON DAILY.

_____

_____

_____

_____

_____

_____

_____

_____

_____

_____

_____

_____

_____

_____

_____

_____

_____

_____

_____

_____

_____

_____

WOMEN AND NO

If women are saddled with tasks of lesser value for career advancement, they have less time for the tasks that are more likely to shine on their evaluation ratings and advance their careers.

It is especially important for women to set boundaries because plenty of research evidence suggests that they are asked (and accept) tasks that perhaps they would be better off not agreeing to. In a fascinating study titled *Gender Differences in Accepting and Receiving Requests for Tasks with Low Promotability,* professor and PhD Linda Babcock of Carnegie Mellon University and her colleagues Lise Vesterlund, Laurie Weingart, and Maria Recalde explore the challenges women face in the workplace. They examined "the allocation of a task that everyone prefers to be completed by someone else (writing a report, serving on a committee, etc.)" to see if women, more than men, volunteer or are asked to volunteer for such tasks. The answer to this question is especially important because if women are saddled with tasks of lesser value for career advancement, they have less time for the tasks that are more likely to shine on their evaluation ratings and advance their careers.

The research findings will not surprise women in the workplace. Women are asked to volunteer for more "low-promotability" tasks than men because it is believed they will accept. And this next point is crucial: women do step up and volunteer to do these tasks. Although the study does not examine why women volunteer more than men, it might be that women find it more difficult to say no, or there is subtle pressure/expectation applied to accept the assignment.

When volunteers are called for assignments that will not have a big impact on career advancement, it is vital that women not fill the void left by the lack of volunteers. In other words, do what many men do: stay silent, which is a form of no when the call for volunteers goes out. Women need to be strategic on what they volunteer for, knowing their day-to-day duties will not be eased. Only say yes to the plum offers that have a higher value and profile within your company.

What if these low-promotability tasks are repeatedly as-*signed* to women rather than offered as a solicitation to volunteer? Here is where women at a workplace need to unite to educate management that change is needed. Documenting and pointing out the inequities could bring about an awareness that fosters a level playing field. It's possible management is not even aware of their tendency to rely on one gender for the more mundane work. Managers might be asking women to fulfill this need simply because they falsely believe women are more suited or want to take on these duties based on the positive response rate. By making management aware of this tendency, the company might pivot to turn-taking rather than assigning or seeking volunteers.

This filling the void by women of tasks that need to be done extends to the home. Too many women put in a full workday for an employer and then shoulder an unfair burden of the household chores (cooking, cleaning, etc.) along with child-rearing (feeding, homework, bath-time, etc.). There's only one way to resolve this inequity: speak up with the power of no. Simply put, couples need to arrive at a fair balance of total hours in a week devoted to work and the same for leisure. The longer a woman goes without raising this need for equitable time, the more entrenched the household pattern is likely to become. If the plea falls on deaf ears, it is time for marriage counseling where an independent counselor becomes the arbitrator. And if you really want to get the attention of your spouse, simply say no to a couple of the extra tasks you do, such as buying the groceries, preparing dinner and/or cleaning the dishes. That should get a response!

TRY IT:

- Step one is recognizing if you are being asked or are volunteering for more than your fair share of assignments. If you are being asked, talk to the person who is doing the requesting and point out that taking turns is a fairer way to proceed. If you are volunteering, save your efforts and be involved in only the "high-promotability" tasks or the type of work you truly enjoy.

- If you are a working woman and doing the lion's share of the housework and child-rearing, it is possible your pleas for fairness fall on deaf ears. You will get your spouse's attention by announcing that you are going on strike if the situation doesn't change: no laundry, no prepared dinners, etc. Most spouses are smart enough to step up before your strike goes into effect.

WRITE THE ONE TAKE-AWAY FROM THIS CHAPTER THAT WILL GIVE YOU THE MOST BENEFIT AND YOU WILL WORK ON DAILY.

_____

_____

_____

_____

_____

_____

_____

_____

_____

_____

_____

_____

_____

_____

_____

_____

_____

_____

_____

_____

_____

_____

_____

IMPULSE

---

*I found the easiest way to correct
my impulse to oblige is to have
a standard response.*

It happens all the time—we say yes to a request, a purchase, or an offer quickly, then we kick ourselves later. Here's a tip from Dr. Vanessa Bohns, who studied just how uncomfortable people are saying no. She points out that the secret isn't moving toward a rote no answer most of the time, but instead "agreeing to things mindfully, rather than because you feel pressured in the moment." And to be mindful of each decision, you might want to buy yourself some time. I have used this technique many times when I can't articulate a good reason for no, and I don't want to try it face to face. My go-to line is either "let me get back to you" or "let me check my schedule." Dr. Bohns adds another option: "Ask the person to send their request via email where you can have some mental space and then craft a thoughtful response."

It's also a good idea to have a go-to scripted no for a request you often get but have difficulty saying no to. Two examples are the frequent requests I get to meet someone for a cup of coffee to discuss their idea for a book I should write or give them tips on how to get published. In the past, my immediate impulse was to be polite and want to accommodate these people. I quickly learned that was a time sucker, a black hole where I felt trapped, and even glancing at my watch didn't send the talker the necessary signal.

I found the easiest way to correct my impulse to oblige is to have a standard response. For the book ideas, my scripted answer is either, "No thank you, I'm already busy with several projects," or "Put your idea in two paragraphs and shoot me an email." I have learned one out of fifty pitches of an interesting story (in my case, survival stories) just might be worth looking into further. Rather than let them tell me the story verbally, I always have them send me a summary. And for the tips about getting published, I refer them to a reference book that does just that. To soften the "no," I explain that's how I learned the business—by reading.

If I had "a quick cup of coffee" with all the people who have asked for advice, I'd have little time for my own projects. Even worse, when I did meet for coffee, the quick meeting dragged on, and I went from feeling like I was helping the person to being resentful that my time was being chewed up.

Despite your best intentions, sometimes you might agree to a person's request in a moment of weakness or because it involves doing them a favor in the future, and you don't give the necessary thought to your impulse to be helpful. Then, as the date gets closer, you have a feeling of dread and stress. You still have an out. We are all allowed to change our minds. You can explain additional demands on your time have come up or you feel uncomfortable with the idea/task and will not be able to assist. This is not the optimal way to exit, but it will serve as a reminder to you that next time you will never accept a request that you truly do not want to do. Instead, you will weigh the consequences of committing to lending a hand. Remember, by saying no to certain people and uncomfortable requests, you preserve time to help those you are closest to.

We mentioned the benefit of email in our quest for freedom, but email also has its pitfalls because of our ingrained impulses. Emails can be misinterpreted more than a verbal exchange, so if an email strikes you as odd or rude, resist the urge to answer immediately and instead pause and let some time pass before responding. I learned this when I once received an email that I thought was condescending, and I instinctively fired back, which led to a nasty exchange of emails. Years later I received an email that I viewed as a personal attack. Instead of letting my impulse get the best of me (think, road rage on a keyboard), I didn't respond until the next day. The email sent to me didn't look so bad after a night's sleep, and my response was low-key and measured.

There was no exchange of nasty emails. And more recently, when I did get a negative email, the best solution was to do nothing. You don't need to take the bait and respond at all.

|||

TRY IT:

- To control your automatic yeses to frequent requests for help, have a scripted response that buys you time or allows for a soft, respectful refusal. Why let your impulse to assist others chew up your free time when you can put the onus on the "asker" and have them put their request or idea in an email? Then you can answer at your leisure.

- Ignore the impulse to lash out against criticism or a perceived attack. Chances are, when you cool down, you can say no to your urge to respond in an overly negative way. Say no to going down the rabbit hole of arguing. Respond in a restrained way, or in some cases, let the negativity fly away and don't respond at all, even if goaded.

KNOW YOUR
OWN IMPULSES

- Is your impulse to always help others? If so, pause and consider the time factor.
- Do you allow yourself time to listen to your gut before answering an invitation or a request? Take a moment to listen to your inner voice's reaction to what is being asked of you.
- Ask yourself how saying yes would affect your stress level.
- Are you sometimes quick to anger, to zip off a nasty response? Next time, practice not replying at all, at least until the next day.

**WRITE THE ONE TAKE-AWAY FROM THIS CHAPTER
THAT WILL GIVE YOU THE MOST BENEFIT AND YOU
WILL WORK ON DAILY.**

_____

_____

_____

_____

_____

_____

_____

_____

_____

_____

_____

_____

_____

_____

_____

_____

_____

_____

_____

EASY NO'S: CREATING MORE TIME FOR YOU

When I reduced these "time-suckers" I had more opportunities to bike ride, take walks, garden, read, make dinner for a friend, take a nap, and more. Just think of the ways you will enjoy more time.

Consider this chapter a pep talk. Most of us realize we have been cramming too much into our lives, which increases our stress level in an era where the pace of change is more rapid than ever, and our menu of options is expanding. We simply have too much on our plates, and we intuitively know that the power of no can set us free, but where do we start?

Let me share some no's that I found were helpful for me. One or two might jump out at you as "easy" no's on your quest to take control of your time. When I undertook the changes outlined below, my goal was to create more opportunities for pursuing hobbies and projects that were important to me. I especially wanted to be in total command of my weekends.

I wanted my weekends to be the sacred time that would energize my family and me.

- **Phone conversations.** Some people drone on, and before you know it, an hour has gone by. They don't pick up on subtleties to wrap up the conversation, so I simply learned to say, "Well, I need to go now." Occasionally, the person would keep talking, and I'd interrupt and repeat that it was time to say goodbye. I honestly believe that by doing that, I "trained" those people to make their calls to me a bit briefer. And remember, just because the phone rings doesn't mean you have to answer it. If you are in the middle of an important task or enjoying a pleasurable pastime or peaceful moment, ignore the call and handle it at your convenience, not theirs.

- **Television.** The average American watches a whopping twenty-eight hours of TV a week. Chances are you are not one of them because you are a reader, but I'll wager that if you keep a record of your TV viewing, the time spent in front of the tube is higher than you thought. I cut my TV watching to a minimum by asking, *Does this passive activity give me pleasure or enhance my life?* Knowing that only a few shows gave me pleasure, I decided that was all I would watch. And the DVR function on the TV, where you can record a show and then watch it later, was a huge benefit. Like the phone call ignored, you can watch the program at the best time for you, not the TV's rating system. Best of all, you can fast forward through commercials and opening credits. (And if you "binge-watch," ask yourself if what you are getting in return for the experience was worth the time.)

- **Social media.** Simply put, do you want to be having your own adventures and accomplishments or watching others post about theirs? Do you need to see when someone has gone to a family gathering or be shown what's on their dinner plate? Staying connected is fine, but limit your screen time, knowing the various platforms, especially YouTube, are designed to suck you in and keep you there. YouTube is downright diabolical, getting you to watch one video after another based on what you have selected in the past.

- **Shopping and clutter.** Shopping can be a huge time-sucker, so only go when you need to and be sure to take a list. The list of items—whether it's the grocery store, a department store, or an online store—will keep you from wandering and looking at items you don't need. And shopping goes hand with clutter: try not to buy another item until you tackle at least one room or one closet of clutter. A good inspiration to help you reduce clutter is the book *The Life-Changing Magic of Tidying Up*. I sometimes struggle with clutter, and

I notice that when things are organized (especially in my office), I can get my hands on what I need faster.

- **News.** However you consume your news, be cognizant that much of what is passed off as news is either speculation or opinion. And if your source is TV, you have probably noticed that what gets shown has more to do with the sensational quality of the video than its importance to world events or impact on your life. I've found that skimming a high-quality, objective newspaper online is a quick way to stay informed. (I also say no to reading or watching on TV long pieces about violent crimes—I don't want to give my time to learn about what a perpetrator did. Why would I want to devote a second to the details about a mentally ill person and their crimes?)

- **Arguing.** When was the last time you won an argument? One person can rarely convince another person to change an opinion through arguing. Having a discussion with a loved one about different solutions to a problem is fine and worthwhile, but when the "discussion" turns to arguing, cut it off. You want to brainstorm, not berate each other.

- **Gatherings.** Not all get-togethers are equal, so pick the ones that fit your schedule and sound like fun, and politely decline the others. Remember that some gatherings, particularly those during the holidays, can be heavy on stress and light on fun. You don't have to go. Some warning factors that you should consider before saying "yes" to the next gathering:

- Does the travel time and congestion make you cringe?
- Will the party be a fun time with an interesting group, or do you suspect one person will dominate the affair?
- Does the preparation add stress? Does it involve purchasing gifts, new clothing, cooking, etc.?

If you feel compelled to go to a function that you aren't looking forward to, remember you can still say no to parts of it: no to overeating, no to excessive drinking, and no to staying longer than an hour or two.

|||

When I reduced these "time-suckers," I had more opportunities to bike ride, take walks, garden, read, make dinner for a friend, take a nap, and more. Just think of the ways you will enjoy more time. Many of our favorite pleasures are simple and don't cost you a dime, but they bring an inner peace just as meaningful as seeing a therapist. You might find yourself trying an activity or tackling an entirely new project and find it so rewarding you can't imagine going back to your old yes habits.

To keep you on track, reset your inner compass with the following three steps:

1. Sear this into your brain: *When I say yes, I will do so mindfully because the request either excites me, intrigues me, or will likely bring me joy.*

2. Now, think of all the things you have said yes to that didn't meet these criteria. Write a few down. This simple process will make you pause at the next request before answering. And if you are unsure, you will say, "I'll get back to you."

3. Remind yourself each day you are on a mission to rebalance your life. You are taking back control of your time by focusing your energy on what's important to you. To do this, you will be selective on what you undertake, and those things you do tackle, you will actually *finish*.

TRY IT:

- Step off the fast track, the yes track, and rediscover that less is more.

- Make a list of the simple pleasures you enjoy but don't seem to have the time for. Keep those firmly in mind next time you find yourself pulled down the rabbit hole of screen time or asked to attend a function that doesn't excite you.

- Experiment with some of the simple time-savers outlined in this chapter for the next two months and keep a journal on how you utilized that freed-up time. Chances are you are going to smile.

CLUES THAT TIME-SUCKERS ARE DOMINATING YOUR WEEKENDS

Do you find yourself on a Sunday evening feeling like you wasted your weekend? Have you won an argument in the past month? Chances are the answer is no and arguing is a waste of your time, trying to convince another you are right. Instead, find a creative way to brainstorm with an individual who is as open-minded as you.

Do you have some fun ideas or learning experiences that you want to have on weekends, but somehow, there is never enough time?

WRITE THE ONE TAKE-AWAY FROM THIS CHAPTER THAT WILL GIVE YOU THE MOST BENEFIT AND YOU WILL WORK ON DAILY.

_____

_____

_____

_____

_____

_____

_____

_____

_____

_____

_____

_____

_____

_____

_____

_____

_____

NO AND YOUR CHILDREN

If you rarely say no and you mean it, your children quickly learn that arguing will get them "no"-where. But if you always say yes and give them whatever they want when they are young, they are going to need you for most everything as they age!

Here's what I learned, and it served my children and me well. Pick your spots. Consider the request. If you are always saying no, chances are that some of those no's are negotiable, and a child knows it. But if you rarely say no and you mean it, they quickly learn that arguing will usually get them "no"-where. However, every now and then, if a child makes a convincing counterpoint, you may want to reconsider. We want our kids to understand their power of mastering verbal skills without shouting, crying, pouting. You want them to use reason. And when they do—and it agrees with your sensibilities—give them a victory once and awhile. I believe that on most requests, parents should be responding with qualified yeses. Or with a "Yes, but first you need to..." (fill in the blank: cut the lawn, take the dog for a walk, etc.). And then, when you say no, you say it with conviction. You never give in because they throw a tantrum.

My philosophy when my kids were younger was to give them as much freedom as possible, which meant letting them have control over many aspects of their lives. For example, their bedrooms were their own—they could decorate or arrange them however they wanted, and I always knocked if the door was closed. They could choose their clothes without me passing judgment. And they could do what they wanted with their hairstyles—if my daughter wanted blue hair, that was her decision, not mine, and if my son wanted hair to his shoulders or a buzz cut, it was his choice to make. I wanted to save my no's for much more important things than fashion.

As your children grow, make sure they earn some of their wants, needs, and possessions. If you give them everything they need when they are young, they will need *you* for almost everything as they age! Your children need some emotional space, problems to solve, and consequences. They get none of that if you say yes to every request for material possessions and you solve every problem. We shouldn't shield children from *all* difficulties. Our job as parents is to raise kids who can do just fine without us. Solving every problem just creates dependency. Doing tasks for a child or teenager out of love or because you can do it quicker or better doesn't help them learn responsibility.

I can think of two incidents with my children that illustrate a couple of these choices children must make. When my two children were about nine and eleven years old, we were shopping, and they wanted me to buy them handheld battery-operated mini fans that also sprayed a mist. I decided this was a good chance for the kids to learn the value of a dollar. (They had plenty of toys and material possessions, so I was not depriving them of something important and therefore no guilt about my decision.) I said, "If you really want those fans, you will have to pay for them out of your savings." They thought about it and said yes, they still wanted the fans. I paid the cashier, and then the kids reimbursed me when I got home. A week later, I asked where the fans were. They said something to the effect they were kind of boring and that one wasn't working. I asked them if they thought the fans were worth the money. They both said, "No way." Years later, we laughed about the fans, although both of my children gave me a hard time for making them pay for them. They did, however, connect the dots to see there was a lesson about impulse buying.

A second instance I recall was my son qualifying for the town's basketball travel team, which only the best players made. All the kids on the team had high skill levels and, of course, the coach gave the most playing time to the best of the best. Consequently, my son sat on the bench during most of the games. One year he didn't try out for the team. Some dads might have said, "Don't give up so easily." But my view was that basketball should be fun, and that meant playing in the games. In his own way, my son showed wisdom—instead of spending another year riding the bench, he participated in a recreational league where he had plenty of playing time. He effectively said no to the time-draining, no-fun travel team and yes to competing in a game he loved.

As parents, we should teach our teenage children about the power of no, particularly when it comes to time management. We all want our children to do well in school or college, and sometimes we become fixated on their academic skill sets and amount of study time. But equally important is the non-academic factor of time management. Researchers Richelle Adams and Erik Blair identified good time management skills as having "a buffering effect on stress and are a key indication of higher performance." While their report was focused on college students, we as parents can help foster this skill earlier by prompting our children to set priorities. And that means helping them say no to every opportunity that comes their way. Like us, our kids are bombarded by stimuli, and asking them to choose what is important to their education and aspirations and what is not helps them establish a lifelong pattern of control.

Time management is not an easy task for teens or young adults when juggling a social life and their studies. But as parents, we can get them started simply by asking them to be aware of what activities are taking up their time, then let them decide which ones are bringing the least amount of satisfaction or are taking up an inordinate amount of time. Ask them to think about what activity *takes the most from you and gives the least in return.* Just opening a dialogue on the subject might cause your child to make small adjustments that lead to big gains academically and a stronger sense of well-being. Studies have shown that the students who perceived they were in control of their time had less tension in their lives and a lower feeling of being overloaded.

TRY IT:

- When your kids are young and want a frivolous item, have them use their own money to purchase it. They quickly learn if their purchase was worth it.

- Initiate discussions with your teens about time management. The whole point is to make them aware of the various uses of their free time. They might surprise you by using the power of no to prioritize what is most important to them.

- Put more emphasis on encouraging a child's *effort* than the outcome. This will foster their sense of self-reliance, and it will show them that not only is failure just a word, it is temporary. (More on "failure" in a later chapter.)

ARE YOU FREQUENTLY TELLING YOUR CHILD HOW BRIGHT AND SMART THEY ARE?

If so, you might be surprised by the findings of a study conducted by Claudia Mueller and Carol Dweck at Columbia University. In their research experiment, one group of children was told how intelligent they were when they completed a task, while another group who completed the same task did not receive praise. The children were then asked if they wanted to do a relatively easy task next or a hard one. Surprisingly, most of the praised children chose the easy task, while many who were not praised chose the difficult task. The praising made the children avoid failure and opt out of challenging problems.

So how should you praise your child? These same researchers conducted more experiments with children. One group was told how smart they were, and the other was complimented for *the effort*. The ones complimented for their effort received better scores and task completion rates than those told they were bright. So, in a nutshell, choose to praise for effort, and your child will be more likely to choose, complete, and even enjoy difficult tasks.

WRITE THE ONE TAKE-AWAY FROM THIS CHAPTER THAT WILL GIVE YOU THE MOST BENEFIT AND YOU WILL WORK ON DAILY.

_____

_____

_____

_____

_____

_____

_____

_____

_____

_____

_____

_____

_____

_____

_____

_____

_____

_____

_____

CAREFUL USE OF NO WITH YOUR RELATIVES AND SPOUSE

If you find a situation is stressful, it's up to you to find alternatives—chances are the other family members are quite happy with the current arrangement.

Saying no to a spouse can be like walking through a minefield. But there is a method that has a fighting chance of success.

How many times have you seen situations where one family member seems to do the lion's share of the work? I've seen this play out when there is an aging parent with multiple children but only one of the siblings becomes the primary caregiver. Where are the other siblings? Is their time more important than the caregivers? The answer is never. Time for all of us is fixed and precious. Often, the caregiver has fallen into the role because they simply didn't say no (or make up an excuse) like the others did. Other times they step up because no one else is. No matter the reason, the person doing all the work should call a meeting and look for an equitable distribution of tasks. If that fails, and the time commitment for the single individual doing the bulk of the work becomes too much, consider having everyone chip in for outside help.

The caregiver example is one of many situations where one person assumes the burden simply because they want to avoid conflict. Say no to that mindset of enslavement. Maybe you're the person that cooks both Thanksgiving and Christmas dinners for extended families. If you love doing it, fine, go to it. But if you find it stressful, it's up to you to find alternatives—chances are the other family members are quite happy with the current arrangement. Instead, propose that everyone brings a different dish of food, or you go out to a restaurant, or each person chip in for a catering service. You get the idea—say no to the status quo if it's not working for you. Your goal is liberation, where you are emancipated from being the primary worker bee.

Be aware of manipulation and those family members who always ask for your time. They will ignore hints that you are not able to do something. You must be direct and clear. You must ask them to listen and not interrupt if you decide to explain your no. Otherwise, some people can go right into a subtle message of giving you a feeling of guilt. They will dangle it like a fisherman does with a worm; it's up to you not to bite.

NO WILL SET YOU FREE

You should help people because you want to, not out of a sense of duty, not out of a fear of losing someone's love or friendship. And if a person repeatedly makes last-minute requests of you because they failed to plan ahead, saying yes only confirms to the requestor that they can continue to do so. In effect, their bad habits spill over into your life, ruining your planning. If you show discipline and foresight, you should expect others to do the same.

Saying no to a spouse can be like walking through a mine-field. But there is a method that has a fighting chance of success. You explain to your spouse or partner that they need to tell you when a request is truly important to them, that you are not great at picking up clues. For example, your spouse says, "Do you want to go to the beach today?" Sounds like a simple invitation that doesn't seem to have a high degree of importance. So, you answer honestly. Maybe you say, "Not today. I want to do such and such." And that should be the end of it. But now assume the requester rephrases the request. "I'd like you to come to the beach with me today. It's my one day off, and I want to spend it with you." My answer: You better get your ass to the beach. Your spouse used language that made it quite clear that the beach is high on their priority list, and they want to spend it (the day) with you.

This technique only works if the two individuals make their intentions clear, and stress that the request is important. A person can't make every wish or appeal imperative, or the partner will soon begin to think all requests are demands. But with practice and open communication, there is no reason for misunderstanding. If something is important, say so; don't assume the other person can read between the lines. Say no to dropping hints.

TRY IT:

- If you are the type of person who wishes to avoid conflict, you might also be avoiding clear and decisive language and assuming others know what you are hinting at. This rarely works—most people will miss your clues and inferences and continue with the status quo. For one month, try coming out of your comfort zone with your spouse and extended family and saying how you feel. You might find a huge burden is lifted from the demands on your time and continued misunderstandings.

- Remind yourself that there are limits to your energy, to your giving. Don't let a sense of duty put a heavy burden on your time when other family members should be doing their part.

- You might be steaming inside because your spouse or family member is doing or not doing a certain thing that is important to you. Ask yourself, *did I make my intention clear?* And if you did let your feelings out in an unambiguous way, and the person has disappointed you, say no to steaming quietly inside. Say yes to explaining exactly what is bothering you. Being direct may not necessarily lead to conflict; the person you are being open with may simply say, "I never realized that; let's try to make it right."

A FEW INDICATIONS THAT YOU MAY NEED TO ALTER CONVERSATIONS WITH SPOUSE OR FAMILY

- Year after year you are the one doing the bulk of the planning, cooking, or hosting at family gatherings.
- You have dropped hints that you are not happy with an aspect of your relationship, but you have never had a sit-down, open face-to-face conversation explaining precisely what the issue is.
- You keep making the same request, and each time the answer is unsatisfactory.
- You have the distinct feeling you are being taken advantage of.

WRITE THE ONE TAKE-AWAY FROM THIS CHAPTER THAT WILL GIVE YOU THE MOST BENEFIT AND YOU WILL WORK ON DAILY.

_____

_____

_____

_____

_____

_____

_____

_____

_____

_____

_____

_____

_____

_____

_____

_____

_____

_____

_____

_____

NO AND YOUR HEALTH

I think of my body as the only vehicle
I'll ever have, and without it being
maintained properly, I won't get far.

Here's an image that if you hold it firmly in your mind and your entire life will improve. Think of a flower with long petals. Each petal represents a different part of your life such as work, your spouse, your children or family, leisure time, your friends, etc. Now at the center of the flower, sometimes called the pistil, is your health. Every part/petal of your life is dependent on your health. The healthier you are, the better those components of your life function and flourish. Yet oddly, so many of us put our health last when it should be first. It's hard to do anything at peak performance and total satisfaction when you feel lousy.

The reason we often put our health last is that we say yes to everything else first. For example: "My workload is nonstop, and I have no time to eat healthy or exercise." What if I told you your work would be less stressful if you flipped that scenario around and put your health first? Think about it. When you are healthy, you have more energy, more focus, and even more creativity. You can accomplish more in a shorter period of time. Your work benefits. And if you think taking time from around the clock demands at your place of employment *might* hurt your chance for a promotion, flip that around and consider that being in poor health with low energy *will most definitely hurt* that promotion possibility.

Another excuse is that your family needs you (to cook, to recreate, to help someone in need). Take a little more time for yourself now and then, and your family will be the beneficiary. You'll be surprised that you can help others more effectively when you're in shape and well rested.

When I don't exercise or eat right or try to get eight hours of sleep, I try to be mindful of the situation and the reasons why I haven't put my health first. Certain images help me right the ship. I think of my body as the only vehicle I'll ever have, and without it being maintained properly, I won't get very far. I remind myself of the good feeling that comes after I exercise from endorphins, instead of the harmful mind weariness/fatigue that comes from juggling too much and being frazzled. Those two thoughts usually prompt me to say *enough* to whatever factors are sucking up my time and instead go outside and hop on my bike for a long ride. For you, your release might be a walk on a quiet road, a wooded path, or along a shoreline. Or maybe it's going to your fitness center where you work up a sweat for at least an hour and then have a healthy meal. Whatever you choose that gets the heart rate pumping, the blood flowing, and helps clear the mind is your path to balance and good health. In effect, you are recharging your vehicle, your body.

Some practical tips to incorporate into your life:

- **Stay hydrated.** Make water your go-to drink. Cut way back on alcohol, sodas, coffee, fruit drinks, and the like. Water has no calories, no sugar, no salts, and chances are, it's free right from your tap. You can occasionally add a little zip to your water by buying a carbonation machine and then squeezing in fresh lime or lemon juice. Say no to the detrimental effects of being over-caffeinated. Say no to obesity and its path to diabetes from sugary drinks. Say no to the harm that more than one alcoholic drink per day can do. (Moderate amounts of coffee, tea, and red wine have beneficial health effects.)

- **Listen to your body.** It tells you when you are exhausted and when your mind has battle fatigue. Slow down for a bit and rest, relax, read, or find the healing power in nature. Anything to lessen the man-made stimuli that bombards us every waking moment. Break the electronic leash now and then.

NO WILL SET YOU FREE

- If you can't do a full workout, **take a twenty- to thirty-minute walk in the fresh air**. It requires no planning, no fees, and no fancy fitness clothes. What you get in return is burned calories, a calming experience, and a chance to look up at the trees, birds, and sky.

- **Develop your exercise routine at home**—you might just cancel your gym membership. Too many people have become brainwashed that they can't work out unless they are at a fitness club. But with the right music to pump you up at home and a couple of pieces of equipment (I use an elliptical machine, some free weights, and a mat for core exercises), you can always squeeze in at least a half hour of exercise when you can't get to your club. You might find working out at home is convenient because there is no driving back and forth. (It always amuses me that most of us park as close as possible to the club entrance to avoid a longer walk, and we then get on a treadmill inside.)

If you are not using your gym membership at least every other day, ask yourself: is it worth it? It certainly is for the gym—they count on people having their monthly membership fee withdrawn from their checkbook but not tying up the exercise equipment because they hardly ever show up. With the money you save from the gym, you could buy some home exercise equipment, a road bike, a mountain bike, a kayak, some snowshoes—and then find an online group to enjoy the activity or enjoy some time alone outdoors.

When we make an effort to put our health and well-being first, we open ourselves up to our full potential. We feel good, and we notice more. I keep a little drawing on the wall I call the gratitude continuum. It starts with my feeling healthy and having a sense of gratitude for the good things in my life. I try to have a sense of childlike wonder and appreciation. That feeling in turn keeps you alert and open to noticing more around you. You become aware of opportunities, take advantage of the ones that feel right, and those opportunities make you feel even more grateful. It all started with our body being as healthy as possible and our minds in a state of grace and gratitude.

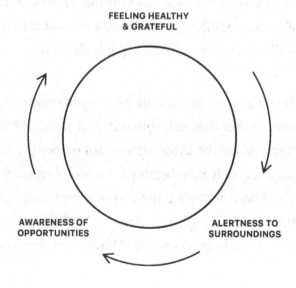

FEELING HEALTHY & GRATEFUL

AWARENESS OF OPPORTUNITIES

ALERTNESS TO SURROUNDINGS

TRY IT:

- You can probably think of many other benefits than the ones listed in this chapter on why you should say yes to your health and no to extreme hours working or other perceived burdens. For one month, try some of the tips I've mentioned with a goal toward more exercise and sleep, along with better nutrition. I'm guessing at the end of a month—even if all you did was take a short walk every day—you would see that being as healthy as you can leads to many side benefits. Keep a journal that chronicles the new healthy steps you're taking. Write down if you think your work or personal relationships have suffered because you carved out some time to nurture your body. With reasonable people, there is usually no downside and only an upside to putting your body first—it's the vehicle that will take you to new heights and adventures.

- In a nutshell, if you can't find time for exercise, proper sleep, and healthy food, it's a clear indication your life is out of balance. Use the power of no to carve out a small block of time for just you and your health by either declining certain demands on your time or cutting back on those demands. A satisfying life or achieving a difficult goal simply can't happen when you feel like crap. Treat your body like a finely tuned, priceless sports car and maintain it the right way so you enjoy the journey to surprising destinations.

- Take a moment to read about the "Blue Zones," those places where people are the healthiest and live the longest. A great book for a primarily plant-based diet (one of the common factors to various Blue Zones worldwide) is *The Blue Zone Kitchen: 100 Recipes to Live to 100*. Just a few of the guidelines at the beginning of the book include:

  - Retreat from meat
  - Go easy on fish
  - Reduce dairy
  - Cut down on eggs
  - Eat a daily dose of beans
  - Slash sugar
  - Snack on nuts
  - Sour on bread (go for sour bread or 100 percent whole wheat)
  - Go whole (avoid as much processed food as possible)

Notice that much of a healthy diet is about saying no to items in the typical American diet and yes to recognizable foods— the way they (vegetables, fruits, nuts, etc.) naturally grow.

DO ANY OF THESE DESCRIBE YOU?

- Overextended
- Weekends are not your own
- You see more fluorescent light than sunlight
- Your schedule is so jammed you could scream
- Your home is a mess

If one or more of these describes your current state, your health is suffering because you have said yes to everything except the most important thing: your well-being. To find the path to a more balanced, less harried life, say yes to taking the time to cook or buy healthy food, exercise, sleep, and more time in nature. All those other components in your life won't suffer from carving out time for your health; they will improve because you will have the energy and calmness to operate at your peak.

WRITE THE ONE TAKE-AWAY FROM THIS CHAPTER THAT WILL GIVE YOU THE MOST BENEFIT AND YOU WILL WORK ON DAILY.

_____

_____

_____

_____

_____

_____

_____

_____

_____

_____

_____

_____

_____

_____

_____

_____

_____

_____

_____

_____

_____

_____

NO WITHOUT SAYING NO
(OR THE ART OF TAKING A PASS)

There are dozens of ways to decline a request without saying no. But in your head, you're thinking, "F**k no," and you will stick to your guns no matter how much pressure or guilt the other person sends your way. Don't let yourself be drawn into a negotiation.

As you take back your time and see the benefits, it will get easier to say no in whatever form works best for you. Just keep reminding yourself, "I am on a mission to simplify my life."

In the first few chapters, you have seen ways to decline demands on your time without ever using the word no. Aside from the quick "no, thank you" to a solicitor calling on the phone, a car salesperson, or an offering of lima beans, our quest to take back your time can succeed without using the word no. "No" is often simply too blunt and viewed as impolite if you give that message to someone you know. This chapter will dive into more ways to convey the same message and get the same results.

Even when you know that you are going to refuse an offer, it helps to listen carefully to the person's request, perhaps ask a question or two, and acknowledge you understand their position (i.e., "Yes, moving from one apartment to another is difficult and stressful; that's why it's best to hire a mover"). This book is not about blowing someone off with a quick rejection, but rather having your priorities rule your decisions and not someone else's. So soften your no by explaining why you cannot accommodate the friend, neighbor, family member, or acquaintance looking for a chunk of your time. Some reliable stand-by responses include:

> "It's not a good time for me right now."
> "I've got too much on my plate."
> "I have a personal policy of not [fill in the blank]."

If you feel a white lie is necessary until you master the art of taking back your time, by all means, use it:

> "I've got a prior commitment."
> "I'm ill-at-ease doing..."
> "I know myself, and I'd be exhausted if I said yes."

Or maybe you feel the situation calls for you to go into a bit more detail.

> "I'm uncomfortable camping in grizzly bear country."
> "My back isn't strong enough to risk injuring it by lifting that."
> "My house isn't set up for company right now."
> "Lima beans make me gag."

You get the picture; there are dozens of ways to decline a request without saying no. But in your head, you're thinking, *F**k no*, and you will stick to your guns no matter how much pressure or guilt the other person sends your way. If the other person continues to ask or picks apart your excuse, move on from giving any more detail and say a firm, unapologetic "no, thank you." Don't let yourself be drawn into a negotiation.

If you use the word no, you can soften it by offering an alternative idea that is more to your liking. An example might be, "No, I don't have time to be one of the fundraiser organizers, but would it be helpful if I reviewed your marketing material?" You've given the requester an offer of limited assistance and now the ball is in their court to say yes or no. The "no, but..." strategy can be used as a crutch with close friends until you feel more confident with a straight-up decline. Or use "no, but" when you truly want to help but in a limited way.

As you take back your time and see the benefits, it will get easier to say no in whatever form works best for you. Just keep reminding yourself *I am on a mission to simplify my life*. You will have some persistent requesters, so be prepared to repeat your declination, each time being clear and concise.

Whenever you are not working for an employer, every bit of your time is owned by you, and nobody can take it away without your approval. But I'm guessing many of you are now asking, "But what about when I'm at work? What about an unreasonable request there?" We will tackle that tricky situation in the next chapter, and you can draw on some of the examples in this chapter of phrasing your desire and opinion without using the word no or being disrespectful.

TRY IT:

- Never answer yes without considering the time factor. Then once you estimate the amount of time you think the commitment might take, double that. I've found almost every task, every obligation, every social occasion lasts far longer than I estimated. And if you are wavering under pressure, at the very least, say, "Let me sleep on it." Being asked to be an organizer of a fundraiser is a serious commitment—there are other ways to help, even if it is simple as saying, "No, but I'll make the first donation."

- Strive to be respectful as you learn the art of no. Even when warning bells are ringing and you want to shout, "F**k no," you can instead pay a compliment. "I applaud your effort and idea, but I can't commit now."

- If an opportunity is offered to you that is quite attractive, but you simply don't have the time, decline it but give a detailed response of your reasons. Sometimes the person doing the asking will adjust the timing for you or make you a counteroffer that involves much less of your time, and your focus is needed only on the part of the offer you like best. I've used this tactic with some interesting business opportunities and been surprised that the asker shows incredible flexibility, and the situation becomes a win-win.

- Don't worry that your no will hurt other people's feelings. First, it's your time, and the other person needs to respect that. And secondly, we tend to believe others will judge us more harshly when we decline their request. Psychologists even have a name for our misguided belief that people will view us negatively when we say no: the "harshness bias." View taking control of your time in a positive light—it's possible others will respect your discipline rather than be disapproving.

- If somehow you got roped into doing something regularly that has consumed way too much time, and you don't want to cut the person off, you can say, "Let's not stick to a schedule." I have a friend who was doing weekly Zooms with another friend and was looking to do far fewer—this moving to a non-schedule might be the way to go.

WRITE THE ONE TAKE-AWAY FROM THIS CHAPTER THAT WILL GIVE YOU THE MOST BENEFIT AND YOU WILL WORK ON DAILY.

_____

_____

_____

_____

_____

_____

_____

_____

_____

_____

_____

_____

_____

_____

_____

_____

_____

_____

_____

_____

NO AT WORK

Saying no to your boss is especially tricky, and the word "no" won't appear in your answer, ever. That doesn't mean you can't negotiate something other than yes. If you are overwhelmed with tasks, it is your responsibility to discuss this with your boss before accepting a new one.

The workplace is fraught with danger for those who use the direct approach of "no." Here, subtlety, tact, and nuance are required. The word no should almost never be used. In the prior chapter, we discussed alternative ways to say no, and in this chapter, we will expand on those while providing some specific examples to use at your place of employment. (For the self-employed, a future chapter will address those challenges.)

The easier no's are to coworkers, and the more difficult ones—the ones that need the most finesse and right delivery—are the situations with your boss or managers higher up the pecking order.

Let's discuss the coworker scenarios first. Certain coworkers are downright annoying and come to you with requests that are not part of your job description. You will probably help them the first couple of times they require assistance, and then in the future explain that you are too busy. But perhaps a better response is to point them to the correct person in the organization who is an expert on that subject. Or maybe there is information online or in a manual that they can review. This is not making excuses. It is helping the requestor by directing them to a person or document more able to assist and get them up to speed.

Sometimes the requestor will be from another department, perhaps recruiting you to contribute to a project where your expertise is needed. Before getting roped in, tell them you need to talk to your manager first. It is important your boss knows who, besides themselves, is directing where your time will be spent.

Saying no to your boss is especially tricky, and the word "no" won't appear in your answer, ever. That doesn't mean you can't negotiate something other than yes. If you are overwhelmed with tasks, it is *your responsibility* to discuss this with your boss before accepting a new one. So set up a meeting to prioritize your work with your manager. It may surprise you when your manager says a task you thought was urgent is no longer a top priority for your boss. And maybe the new project given to you—once you discuss it—is not as onerous as you thought or has a deadline far enough out that you think you can make it. Still another option is that after you explain how all your other work will suffer because of the new task, you could be involved as an expert on your line of work as needed. That is far better than accepting full responsibility and then not being able to deliver. Good managers will value someone who is assertive, honest, and offering alternatives.

The conversation is the key—now your boss will at least think before assigning you yet another task. Don't wait until you are in meltdown mode and doing a lousy job on every task because you have been assigned so much work. Communicate.

Another tack to use with your boss when you feel you cannot take on any more work is to point out that by working on yet another project, the quality will not be up to your (or their) standards and that you will be jeopardizing the delivery and value of existing projects. Hopefully, this statement will force your manager to reevaluate all the work on your plate, and you should encourage them to review each task with you one by one. The simple act of diving into each assignment might open your boss's eyes to the fact that you are overloaded, and perhaps a project or two can be reassigned or put on the back burner. Again, it's the employee's responsibility to open the dialogue and not to say yes to every demand just to please the boss. In my prior corporate experience, I learned that trying to do it all can be a recipe for disaster as the quality of your work goes down while your resentment builds. Try talking it out.

If you are a hard worker and a valued employee, it's possible to set some boundaries without pissing off management—they won't want to lose you. For example, if you have been answering work-related emails almost immediately every night and during the weekend, you might want to set aside some of that time for family or simply for yourself. You might explain to your boss that to avoid burnout, you won't be answering emails on a Sunday unless it is labeled "emergency," and it truly is one.

Another scenario is if you are a parent and you're never home in time for the family dinner. Carve out at least a couple of days a week where you guarantee the family you will be there. That might mean arriving at the office at 6:00 a.m. (and making sure through email that your boss knows), and leaving in time for dinner. And if someone schedules a meeting for late in the day, and you have to be at that meeting, first try to get the meeting rescheduled, and if that doesn't work, let everyone know what time you have to leave for an "appointment." Fortify your resolve by telling yourself that your kids will never be this age again, and you owe it to them, your spouse, and yourself to share this time where you are all together. And if you feel your work situation simply won't allow this family time, something is seriously wrong, and you should commit within the next six months to either carve out the family time or find a company that understands work-life balance. Say no to being a slave and waking up someday and seeing your kids are grown and don't care about spending time with you.

Even now, while I'm self-employed, I consider some of the publishers and publication editors I write for as my bosses, and I try to give great service. But every now and then, I'll get an urgent request to complete something immediately because *they* have fallen behind or are feeling the pressure. On one request that I certainly did not feel was an emergency, I did not even try to meet their deadline. Before I found the time to start the task, I received an email from that person, saying never mind, they solved the problem. In that case, my delay made the urgent request disappear. My takeaway was something I've known for many years: certain people love to transfer their stress as if it's a baton in a relay race. In this instance, I simply didn't take the baton.

If your boss is incorrigible (one who says almost every task is a top priority) and you see little hope for a change in managers, start planning your escape. It may take months or even a year, but you are saying no to poor management with no empathy. In the meantime, just keep doing your best. If you can look in the mirror and know you're giving your job 100 percent effort (and not jeopardizing your health), what more can you ask of yourself? Hang in there and keep looking for a new position. There are plenty of managers and companies who will provide clear direction while showing true appreciation for the skills and dedication you offer.

Almost as frustrating as the managers who won't even listen when you are overwhelmed and give you the rote response of "multi-task" are the bosses who are so narrow-minded that they reject every new idea you offer. Managers can become so entrenched in the status quo they sometimes brush aside an idea that is clearly a time saver that streamlines operations. Again, if there is no hope for a change in managers in your department, start the search for a new position within or outside the company. You don't want to spend years working for someone who operates out of fear of experimenting with a new concept because they don't want to rock the boat. Those managers are creativity killers. You want to be in an environment where improvements in workflow and process are possible rather than shot down out of habit.

Since this book is all about time management, I must comment on meetings. I've given seminars to business groups about conducting a productive meeting, and if I had to boil down the three most essential factors, they would be:

1. Have an agenda distributed before the meeting, and make sure people stick to only what's on the agenda.

2. Do not attend a meeting that doesn't have an end time. If no end time is given in the agenda, ask when the meeting will be over because you need to plan your day. Little is accomplished when the meeting lasts more than one hour.

3. Everyone should have a chance to speak without being interrupted, but there should be a strict time limit for each person—without it, you can be sure one person will drone on and on. And say no to anyone who is trying to poach an idea that you originated. Stop them in their tracks and say, "I said the same thing a few minutes ago," or "I've already written and distributed that idea a while ago." Say no to anyone trying to steal your thunder.

4. Near the end of the meeting, the meeting organizer should summarize what needs to be done next and who is expected to do what and when. After the meeting concludes, they should type up the summary and deliver it to everyone.

One last work-related issue: raises and promotions. My approach? The answer is always no if you don't ask (and, of course, have a list of accomplishments). I take the "always ask" approach to almost every facet of my life. And I'm often shockingly surprised when some of the long-shot things I've asked for are granted. There is rarely a downside to asking, and sometimes a nice surprise. Even perfect strangers have accommodated me because I took the time to ask respectfully. (Who knows, maybe they said yes because they were too uncomfortable saying no and had not read this book!)

Before asking for a raise, it is important to know your value. How do you do that? You interview with other companies. You will get offers for a competitive wage or salary higher than where you currently work, which is the ammunition you need with your employer. You also want to *make your managers dependent on you*, so they do everything in their power to keep you. It is also important to pick the right time to discuss a raise or a promotion. You want to do it when your stock is up and when you have made a real effort to be noticed. Don't assume that just by working harder, your bosses will notice. It's up to you to say no to being a wallflower and yes to having your successes and contributions be broadly seen.

TRY IT:

- Keep track for a month of how many hours you work per day, including all the emails and phone calls you receive at home and all the family dinners you missed. When I worked in corporate America, I found this a good practice to force me to carve out time for myself. And if you don't believe we Americans are overworked, just look at these data points:

    ○ According to the **ILO** (International Labor Organization), "Americans work 137 more hours per year than Japanese workers, 260 more hours per year than British workers, and 499 more hours per year than French workers." And the average US employee now works the equivalent of an extra month per year compared to what we did in the 1970s. The US is the *only* country in the Americas without a national paid parental leave benefit. The average is over twelve weeks of paid leave anywhere other than Europe and over twenty weeks in Europe. And the list of other metrics illustrating how we in the US work around the clock goes on and on. Say no to giving every waking hour to your job rather than your health and family.

- Make a habit of interviewing at another company every six months. This is the only way to know your true value. With that knowledge, you will be in a much stronger position when it comes to raises and promotions.

DOES THIS SCENARIO SOUND FAMILIAR?

Your manager comes to you with a new assignment, and they say, "This is high profile, so get right on it." The same manager comes with another project, this time explaining, "Senior management needs this soon." Next, there is a third project, this one described as "Crucial to meet our client's needs, so a quick turnaround is important. When the fourth assignment comes, you still have not completed the first one, but this latest one "needs to be done ASAP but be thorough."

Some managers do this "urgent overload" without even realizing it. But you can see the problem with this scatter approach: each assignment is of the utmost importance, and it's up to you to force a prioritization with your manager before you drown. If you have little hope they will give clear direction but are heavy on the BS, then you should prioritize them as best you can and send the prioritization to your manager, saying here is how you will tackle them, and they should let you know if they would rather see the order changed. You haven't said no to any of the projects, but you have developed a game plan.

PS: When you prioritize, put the high recognition project first—it is the one that will get you noticed by senior management, and down the road, it might be your ticket to a new position.

**WRITE THE ONE TAKE-AWAY FROM THIS CHAPTER
THAT WILL GIVE YOU THE MOST BENEFIT AND YOU
WILL WORK ON DAILY.**

_____

_____

_____

_____

_____

_____

_____

_____

_____

_____

_____

_____

_____

_____

_____

_____

_____

_____

NO TO NEGATIVITY

Randomness does occur in both good ways and bad; the key is what you do with it. I choose to minimize the bad luck, trying to learn and make something positive out of it.

One of the worst things that can happen in an author's career is having a publisher hold the rights to a book you slaved over, then perpetually postpone the publication date. That happened to me years ago, and you would think nothing good could come out of the situation. That is certainly how it looked to me. Even after I went to small claims court and won the battle, and the rights reverted to me, I still was down about the whole experience and didn't have much enthusiasm looking for a new publisher. Then a wonderful thing happened that has helped me in future predicaments where everything seems to go wrong. I not only found a new publisher for three of my books, but I also found one of my best friends for the past twenty-two years.

Adam, my new publisher, became my fishing pal and one of my closest confidants. During our friendship, we have helped each other through many of life's minefields, from divorce to health issues. I tell this little story because I would never have met Adam if the initial publisher had fulfilled their part of our agreement. I now know that no matter how bad a situation looks, it's quite possible—no, probable—that with the right attitude, something good will arise from it. And that knowledge, during times of a difficult ordeal, keeps my negative thoughts to a minimum while I remind myself *good things are coming.*

How about the negative thoughts you have in your head? The cure: practice optimistic self-talk. Do it often. It can be as simple as, "Every day I get stronger, smarter, better, moving me one step closer to (fill in the blank)." Practice positive self-talk, and it will help crowd out the negative thoughts. And if practice and frequency don't work, try a few sessions with a therapist, particularly a cognitive-behavioral therapist who can help transition you from the negative voices in your head to the positive ones. Just a few visits to a good therapist can get you on the right path, a path that you stay on for the rest of your life.

When bad stuff happens in your life, remember that good things will soon come your way if you put the effort in. This can be hard when you're in the middle of a rough situation, but by filling your head with positive talk and *believing* that you can make the best of a bad situation, this soon becomes your mindset for every disappointment. Now, on any setback, I say, *Mike, make something out of this—an opportunity will soon show itself.* One of the convictions I learned that helps keep me on this positive path during big disappointments is a line my daughter wrote to me: "Just remember the dots don't connect looking forward, only backward." She is a wise person, knowing that you grow by things that are difficult and not easy, and it takes time to see the positive you can coax out of a negative.

Author and psychologist Dr. Richard Wiseman explains that you can teach yourself to become more "lucky," and that it is attitude and outlook rather than a mysterious force. When a bad event or accident befalls someone who views themselves as lucky, they always look at the bright side of the situation and acknowledge it could have been much worse. Wiseman says people who view themselves as lucky "expect the best and it becomes a self-fulling prophecy. They are prepared to move in directions they didn't intend; they are flexible people." So if you have negative thoughts and consider yourself unlucky, try to mentally flip that switch and expect the best. That, in turn, can put you in a better mood, and because you are less anxious and maybe even relaxed, you see more of what's happening around you and are prepared to capitalize on the opportunity. His research supports my motto of positive self-talk and my practice of knowing that one way or another, I'll make something good come of a situation. My experience with the bad publisher leading to my friendship with Adam was just the start of my belief that I can help create good things if I keep an open mind and consider myself "lucky" in every endeavor. That, in turn, has allowed little things, like the cancellation of an outing or a planned event, to roll right off my back and think, *I'll be on the lookout, and something even better is going to happen.* On bigger setbacks, I use the self-talk to say no to self-pity and negativism and keep optimistic that I will soar to my natural state of independence once again. I'll block out the naysayers and instead think my imagination is the only limit to what might happen.

One example where I helped chance along was the Disney movie based on my cowritten book, *The Finest Hours.* When people say how lucky I am, I always agree and express gratitude that chance shined down on me, and the stars aligned. But one thing I should begin to add to my response is that "I helped luck along." By that, I mean that I increased my odds of having a book made into a movie by writing *several* books about historical rescues, thereby increasing my odds that one of them would catch the attention of a producer and film studio. And the co-author and I spread the word about *The Finest Hours* story whenever and wherever we could, again helping to make some luck. You never know who might be listening.

Randomness *does* occur in good and bad ways; the key is what you do with it. I choose to minimize the bad luck, trying to learn and make something positive out of it. I tell myself something good will come of it, and that given time, it will all work out for the better. This attitude sets me up to *look* for a positive prospect, and sure enough, something happens to pick me up. And when I see a glimpse of an interesting opportunity, I kick the door open, hoping to experience joy from the good fortune before it slips away.

How about negativity from other people? Here are four guidelines I have found helpful:

1. Don't try over and over to change another person's negativity. I used to make several attempts to point out to another person what seemed like a clear way for them to solve their problem. Now, after one or two shots with no sign of action on their part, I understand they will only change when they want to and when they are ready.

2. Say no to people that manufacture drama. I've noticed the less a person has going on in their life, the more they dwell on a couple of relatively minor misfortunes. Their griping can exhaust and drain you of your vitality and enthusiasm. And sometimes, they want to pull you into their whirlpool of woe. Stay out of that current so you don't get sucked in.

3. Don't give away your power and energy to a negative person or even a negative experience. If you or a friend continually talk about something bad that has happened, you are giving that event more prominence.

4. Stay away from "places of negativity." By that, I mean those mediums that make their money by being negative such as cable news and talk radio. And sometimes, a place of negativity is a physical place. In one corporate job I held, that place was the lunch table. Once I realized the conversations were mostly negative (often about our jobs), I found it healthier to take a walk at lunch or scoot to the public library nearby to hunt for interesting books.

If you are reaching for a new goal, one that is difficult and involves courage, plenty of people will point out the long odds or the impossibility of the dream ever happening. Their intentions may be with your best interest in mind, but their response to your effort is still negative rather than one filled with support and helpful tips. "Naysayers," said Arianna Huffington, "have little power over us—unless we give it to them."

Safeguard your goals, self-confidence, and dreams from those who take the energy out of the room. Instead, gravitate toward people who listen, people who brainstorm positively and unconventionally. You can be practical and still achieve your dreams—and your path is made easier by those who understand what you're trying to accomplish and cheer even your smallest of successes.

TRY IT:

- For two weeks, practice positive self-talk. Strive to be your best every day and push out negative thoughts by saying, "Each day, I'm getting stronger and moving toward my goals. I don't know when I'll get there, but I'm going to enjoy the journey and learn along the way." I'm betting that after the two weeks are up, you'll feel a little stronger, more confident, and discover some insights into how to recreate yourself into the real you. And don't forget to say no to the "time-sucking" things in your life and instead put your energy into what matters most to you first.

- Cast off your lines to toxic people in your life, the ones who can't seem to control a negative reaction to so many of life's little troubles. Their energy field is one of bitching and complaining. Now think of the people you know who are the opposite; they laugh often and energize you with enthusiasm. Spend more time with them and find others of similar makeup, and you will see their outlook will soon become part of your own.

- Tell yourself repeatedly that you are a lucky person and that because of your flexibility, you will always be on the lookout for opportunities and new experiences. Discard self-defeating talk after a setback that might say, "Stuff like that always happens to me." Throw out phrases that tie you to predictable and disappointing outcomes such as, "That's just who I am" or "I'm too old for [fill in the blank]" or "I could never...." When setbacks occur, transition from the initial disappointment to believing that something good will come out of the experience. Make your mindset one of flexibility, that you are still growing as a person and now perceive life as full of interesting surprises.

- Be aware of when you complain about fatigue or ailments. By talking about them frequently, you give them more power and they take up an unwelcome part of your waking thoughts. Save your discussion of minor physical disorders for your doctor, or, even better, start the steps that you know can help alleviate the discomfort.

**WRITE THE ONE TAKE-AWAY FROM THIS CHAPTER
THAT WILL GIVE YOU THE MOST BENEFIT AND YOU
WILL WORK ON DAILY.**

_____

_____

_____

_____

_____

_____

_____

_____

_____

_____

_____

_____

_____

_____

_____

_____

_____

_____

_____

_____

_____

_____

_____

A NEW TAKE ON "FAILURE"

*I try not to view a failure in a negative
light, but instead learn from it and
continue on my way to fulfillment.*

Sometimes we make the mistake of classifying difficult experiences or failed attempts as bad things. Trust me—for every successful book I've had, I've also got at least two projects that never saw the light of day. When I started writing, I received rejection letter after rejection letter. But here's the thing—I didn't view them as failures. Instead, I considered them free advice (if I agreed with their insights) and part of the bigger learning process. You can do the same with criticism.

First ask yourself, *is it true?* The criticism that rings true offers you suggestions to improve, and the ones that don't make sense to you, well, flick those away like a piece of lint and forget about them. Either way, you're not wasting time; instead, you are agreeing or disagreeing and moving on. A mental image I use in such situations is that I'm going down a river with whitewater in my kayak, and I'm bound to hit some rocks or brush up against a snag. I expect that to happen, and sometimes it's because of my poor reading of the river, but no matter the cause, I bounce off the obstruction and continue on my way to my destination that we'll call the "fulfillment town."

I learned that people succeed not because they are brighter or more talented than others but because they are more productive. By having more irons in the fire (for me, it was books and articles and a quest to expand friends), I had more opportunities for attainment. I might have had a high failure ratio, but I also had plenty of hits and even home runs. I always knew my productivity and drive—more than my talent—would get me to my goals. Later, I confirmed this in various studies of those who wash out of difficult programs/goals and those who ultimately succeed. The process is chronicled in-depth in an interesting book titled *Grit*, written by Angela Duckworth, PhD in psychology. Her studies reveal that persistence and dogged determination are better indicators of success than pure talent and smarts.

Successful people often have far more failures than the average person, simply because they keep trying new things and they quickly bounce back from flops and botched attempts. The keyword here is *attempts* because that's what successful people do—they keep at it, they keep tweaking their approach, and are naturally curious. In essence, they say no to failure because they don't let it derail them from whatever it is they are pursuing. Failure doesn't keep them down because they expect problems and address them. They don't necessarily solve the problem, but that's okay because they find another path forward. Sometimes you have to go around a problem rather than unravel it and proceed through it.

By coincidence, as I write this chapter, I'm reading the autobiography of Oscar-winning director and screenwriter Oliver Stone, and boy, did he have failures before finally hitting his stride. Regarding his early screenplays, he said, "I grew a file with dozens, probably hundreds, of written turndowns, a dossier of shame, from which I drew hurt and a perverse pride in being able to take rejection." There's a lot to think about in that sentence. Yes, rejection stings at first, but to me, the important aspect is that he could "take rejection" and keep producing. And produce he did; early efforts were flops, but each time, he learned something new from the process. The man with hundreds of turndowns created *Midnight Express*, *Platoon*, *Salvador*, *Scarface*, *JFK*, *Wall Street*, and many more hits.

In a prior chapter, I mentioned the studies conducted by Dr. Richard Wiseman, and he has this to say about failure in the workplace: "Encouraging people to fail [is important] ... we want people who are prepared to take sensible but realistic risks." His research also reveals that visualizing the steps necessary to reach a goal is far more important than visualizing the result. My research, working with survivors who have achieved what most of us consider impossible, backs this up. Their focus was laser-sharp on the two or three steps they thought they needed to take to keep going, rather than spending time thinking about the ultimate result. I call this "the power of little steps." They can add up to an outcome that seems near impossible. Action is needed in difficult situations, rather than dwelling on the final goal, which can seem out of reach. If you only focus on the result, it's easy to be overwhelmed thinking of what a long shot it might be. Better to start implementing those little steps and inching toward the objective.

Author Wayne Dyer defines an intelligent person as one who chooses happiness. And that intelligence shows up in the face of adversity: "You can begin to think of yourself as truly intelligent," says Dyer, "on the basis of how you choose to feel in the face of trying circumstances." Another Dyer quote I love is, "Those who recognize problems as a human condition and don't measure happiness by an absence of problems are the most intelligent kind of humans we know; also, the most rare."

So don't avoid failure and setbacks, but accept them as part of life, as part of the journey to self-improvement or a particular goal. Your goal can be fixed, but your path to get there should be flexible and fluid because *you will* experience big bumps in the road. It's up to you to either solve the problem, change direction, or modify the plan.

Failure can have yet another positive result: it can increase our empathy for others who have hit a rough patch and restore our sense of humility if needed. We all know some successful people who have become arrogant and selfish—a setback might be the wake-up call they need.

When disappointment, failure, or setbacks come, sometimes the best approach is to recognize the situation's absurdity, even the incredible bad luck that might have caused it. In a few of my setbacks I even learned to laugh at the situation and find the humor in the ludicrous series of events cascading down on me. If you can occasionally chuckle at a setback, imagine how you can laugh at something silly, witty, or that strikes you as ludicrous. You want to develop your laughing the same way you would staying in shape or eating right—nurture it until it becomes part of your everyday life, so that it crowds out that place in your mind that once held negative thoughts. Laughter is its own medicine to help relieve stress and forget yourself for a few moments. And it makes you feel damn good. Imagine the life you could live if you laugh at some frustrations that made you angry or sad.

Larry David (*Curb Your Enthusiasm* and *Seinfeld* producer) is an expert at coaxing laughter from the mundane. He illustrates the humor in everyday scenarios of life that have a touch of absurdity—the things that don't go as planned. The other person that comes to mind is Norman Cousins. In his book *Anatomy of an Illness*, he described how, when he had a rare disease, a big part of his healing process was immersing himself in movies, comedian performances, and books that made him laugh. I make a determined effort to do the same, but I add friends who make me laugh to that list.

With enough practice, you can change your outlook on what other people call failure. Say no to thinking that failure is an ending, and instead consider it a mere bump in the road or a detour. And who knows, someday you might even see the humor in some of those bumps and continue on your way to "fulfillment town."

TRY IT:

- Say no to the traditional way most people view failure and instead view setbacks as part of the process of discovery. Many highly successful people have had multiple failures, but they continue to produce and probe in new directions until they hit their stride.

- Acknowledge *your* role in some mistakes, learn from them, and then move on, rather than dwelling on the disappointment. You will soon learn to forgive yourself quickly and not look to blame others for the hurdles in your path.

- You or others might have labeled a particular event a failure. But what if that concept is only inside your brain? What if it is an imposter and not a failure, but a simple event that prompts you to alter your path? Try looking at a couple of recent scenarios that you thought were disasters in a new light and ask yourself were they failures or temporary surprises that you didn't like at the time. Chances are we have overblown the significance of something we initially labeled a failure and instead was a minor detour from which we learned.

BECOMING A LUCKY PERSON EVEN WHEN FAILURE KNOCKS YOU DOWN

I read *The Luck Factor* by Richard Wiseman when it first came out in 2003 and found that it reinforced principles I try to live by. Rereading the book recently, I realized I'd strayed a bit from the ideas Wiseman shares from his years of scientific study into why some people seem luckier than others. Wiseman concludes that people are not born lucky but incorporate a few basic strategies into their lives, sometimes without even knowing it. One of the principal techniques involves how lucky people can transform bad luck into good fortune. Wiseman explains that they do so in the following ways:

1. Lucky people see the positive side of their bad luck.
2. They are convinced that, in the long run, their ill fortune will work out for the best.

3. They do not dwell on their ill fortune.
4. They take preventive measures to keep the event from happening again.

The Luck Factor is an insightful book that I highly recommend, particularly if you feel you are not a lucky person.

WRITE THE ONE TAKE-AWAY FROM THIS CHAPTER THAT WILL GIVE YOU THE MOST BENEFIT AND YOU WILL WORK ON DAILY.

_____

_____

_____

_____

_____

_____

_____

_____

_____

_____

_____

_____

_____

_____

_____

_____

_____

_____

_____

_____

NO WILL SET YOU FREE

THE THREE P'S: PERFECTIONISM, PROCRASTINATION, AND PATTERNING

Say no to the phrase and mindset "I'll be happy when…." That thought of waiting for things to be just right or near perfect is a foolish way to live your life. You're giving up the sure thing (the present, today) for unsure (some future tomorrow), which may never come.

Considered the best gymnast in the world, Simone Biles shocked that world when she pulled out of many Olympic events in 2021. In a nutshell, Biles said no to perfectionism and other people's expectations and yes to her well-being. Anticipation for Simone to achieve medal after medal was through the roof, and many people began to think her incredible athletic displays were a given. But they forgot she is human, no different than the rest of us, and not a machine that can churn out precision day in and day out.

"We also have to focus on ourselves," said Biles during the Olympics, "because, at the end of the day, we're human too, so we have to protect our mind and body rather than just go out there and do what the world wants us to do."

I, for one, felt a surge of pride for Simone Biles when I read those words. She would not let pressure from anyone force her to do something that simply did not feel right. I applaud her for not risking injury to meet others' expectations. It takes a strong person to do that on the world stage. She explained how her timing had not been sharp during practices, causing her to "get lost" in the air on some of her events like the vault.

"It's honestly petrifying trying to do a skill but not having your mind and body in sync."

She had already proven to the world she was the best at what she did, and now she proved her courage differently—making the difficult decision to put herself first. By doing that, she also shed new light on mental health, not only with athletes but with all of us, especially those who strive for perfection. We are imperfect creatures, period. Sure, we can try to attain our best selves and be at peak performance, but it's impossible to deliver it day in and day out.

Multiple Olympic Gold Medalist Michael Phelps, commenting on Biles, said it best: "We need to spend more time on mental health. It's OK to not be OK. Sometimes I felt like a zoo animal." I'm sure Naomi Osaka, the world-class tennis player, concurs. She too made a stand for her mental health in 2021 by first pulling out of the French Open after refusing to attend a press conference because of her "social anxiety" and then dropping out of Wimbledon. She said no to the expectations that she could grind through one tournament after another and ignore the stress and its manifestations. Instead, she said yes to taking some time off and focusing on feeling better.

Biles's and Osaka's decisions are a great reminder for all of us that we can take a step back from time to time. We will not always be at the top of our game, and sometimes, it's best to pause and let others take over. And that is what Biles did—she didn't run and hide but instead was in the stands at the Olympics cheering on her teammates.

| | |

With the media bombarding us with glamorous people leading extraordinary lives, I can understand how a young person can compare their existence and think, *My life sucks.* But trust me when I say nobody's life is perfect, no matter how dazzling the media makes it out to be. Don't compare yourself to others: not monetarily, not with appearance, and not with careers. Follow your compass on what makes you happy and what future goals work best for you. Say no to the phrase and mindset "I'll be happy when...." To me, that thought of waiting for things to be just right or near-perfect is a foolish way to live your life. You're giving up the sure thing (the present, today) for the unsure (some future to-morrow), which may never come. The key is to enjoy the journey on your way to fulfilling a dream or a goal.

I've quoted many modern-day people in this book, but here's one from the distant past written by Seneca in 65 AD: "The greatest loss of time is delay and expectation which depend on the future. We let go the present which we have in our power and look to the future which depends on chance—and so trade a certainty for an uncertainty."

I I I

Say no to ruminating about falling short of your lofty standards. It doesn't matter whether it's you who pushes yourself to be perfect or if you think others require you to be flawless. Either way, it is not a healthy path. Psychologist Gordon Flett studied people who were perfectionists and was featured in *Discover* magazine. He found that those striving for perfection often feel self-conscious and brood about the need to be flawless. They often feel, said Flett, "that they're not as good as others." Flett and other researchers concluded that perfectionism could lead to "imposter syndrome," where you are afraid you will be exposed as unworthy and doubt your accomplishments.

| | |

On a different note, I believe there is a strong connection between perfectionism and procrastination. I've seen it first-hand with people saying, "I've always wanted to write a book." Often, when I ask them if they have tried, they answer yes, but they gave up. I ask why and they say something like, "I couldn't get past the first page or two; the writing wasn't where it should be." My answer is always the same: "It doesn't have to be perfect. Just get it going and keep it flowing, and then go back and make it as good as you can. It's likely never going to be perfect in your mind, but it will improve as you work on it."

Time and again, I've seen people—not just writers—sit on the sidelines rather than participate in something because they were not stellar, elite, or expert at the activity. That leads to a life of loneliness. Here's one last example. I stink at golf. But I refuse to let that keep me from occasionally playing with friends. I know I'm bad, I know I won't put the time into becoming good, but I'm not going to let that stop me from enjoying the sport. And I do enjoy golf because I put no pressure on myself and laugh as I'm playing. I'm not going to let being "bad" at an activity I enjoy stop me from participating.

This advice could be applied to any endeavor you try: don't let self-analysis lead to paralysis. Get started on the project, and new ideas and techniques will bubble up and improve what you're working on. In the *Discover* magazine article mentioned earlier, the author Agata Boxe does a fantastic job discussing perfectionism because she considers herself a recovering perfectionist. Boxe related how the fear of not hitting her unreasonable standards stalled her writing process. "It sometimes made me miss deadlines ... Grades below an A-minus often sent me into despair." She explained how she sometimes avoided interactions with other people because of her perfectionism. Boxe cited studies of others struggling for perfection, saying they "did not like to admit their shortcomings [and] were more prone to feeling uneasy about interpersonal interactions."

But there is hope when you recognize your tendencies toward perfectionism. Boxe ended her article by explaining that during a job search for an academic position, she was too tired to be perfect. "I no longer attempted to hide my flaws. I took a chance to be myself and talked about how I tried to manage my time but sometimes failed. It worked. I got the job." (Little does she know that I thought her article in the magazine was perfect. I wished I had written it!)

III

The final P in this trilogy is patterning. This occurs when we take a narrow view and think there is only one path to a goal. We model our steps precisely like those who have gone before us, imitating what we think is a one-size-fits-all design that we need to follow. Say no to that kind of approach; there might be a better way that fits your skills and your personality. Forcing yourself to follow a pattern can also lead to procrastination because if the model doesn't work for you, delay can occur.

One of the best examples of someone who said no to the established route to a goal was NBA basketball star Kevin Garnett. In his book *KG, A to Z*, he tells a wonderful story of how his dyslexia during his senior year in high school made taking the SATs and ACTs especially difficult. But he thought his only choice was to get into college and play there and then hopefully go on to the NBA. One day, he and a friend snuck into the Chicago Bulls practice facility and were in the stands watching Michael Jordan and Scottie Pippen.

A security guard motioned Garnett down to the court, and KG did as he was told. Jordan greeted him with a terse, "Let's just go. You guard Scottie." The whole scene was a bit unreal for KG as he began playing ball with his idols—and he held his own.

The story gets more amazing. During a break in the games, another basketball legend, Isiah Thomas—recently retired from the Detroit Pistons, not the Bulls—happened to be at the practice facility and strolled over to Garnett after the scrimmage. KG wasn't sure why Thomas was even there, but he was even more surprised when he said, "You could play in the league right now." It's an epiphany for Garnett: he realized the NBA was within his grasp. Thomas then asked, "Well, what do you think? You ready to go into the league?" KG explains in his book that was the moment his path forward became clear, and he said yes. The next lines he wrote were the most interesting: "And after those yeses came no. No to the SATs, ACTs, and college. No, I didn't have to follow a twenty-year-old template." The rest is history: KG entered the draft right out of high school and had a hall-of-fame career.

Is something holding you back? Is it perfectionism? Procrastination? Or maybe you think you must follow a certain path? Chart your own course, and don't wait for everything to be perfect.

TRY IT:

- If you think you fall into the category of someone who is always on a quest for perfection, take a step back and ask yourself if that is a healthy outlook. Is fretting over the smallest of screw-ups worth it? Is stressing daily how you want to live? If the answer is no, which I hope it is, acknowledge that while you should strive to do your best, effort will often fall short of your lofty standards, and that's okay.

- Break yourself of the desire to pattern your life after others. When I was young, I remember thinking, *marriage by age thirty, a house by thirty-two, kids by thirty-five*, and on and on. After all, that's what most of my peers were doing. But I quickly learned it's much more important to do what works best for you.

PROCRASTINATION CURE = JUST GET STARTED!

Taking the first step is the key. It won't be
perfect; there will be false starts and stops,
but get started, and the rest will flow. This
approach is like the saying that showing up is
half the battle.

**WRITE THE ONE TAKE-AWAY FROM THIS CHAPTER
THAT WILL GIVE YOU THE MOST BENEFIT AND YOU
WILL WORK ON DAILY.**

NO IS NOT SELFISH

I find that when I've carved out time for myself and am not harried or feeling rushed, I'm a much better listener.

When we were children, we were taught to be "good," get along with others, be kind, be respectful, and so on. Many of us internalized that to mean that, whenever possible, we should agree with others and make ourselves available when asked to do something. And as we grow up, we don't want to hurt other people's feelings by not fulfilling a request. So many of our actions are taken to avoid the interpretation of being "selfish." Well, throw that thinking out the window. The opposite is true: saying no has nothing to do with self-ishness and everything to do with finding the balance to make you relaxed and happy. And when that happens, you are a more giving, thoughtful, and empathetic person. When you feel an inner calmness, you are better equipped to help others in need. But first, you need to focus on yourself.

Every time you say no to requests that feel like a burden, you create time to say yes to what's important, special people, and your passions. When you discover the limits of how much you can pack into a week, a more peaceful, generous you emerges, and everyone benefits. Maybe instead of going to a party or function you secretly dread, use that time to volunteer for a cause where your time can truly make a difference. Nothing selfish about that.

I find that when I've carved out time for myself and am not harried or feeling rushed, I'm a much better listener. I put more effort into understanding what the other person is truly trying to convey. The relaxed Mike doesn't interrupt but rather is more compassionate and caring. I want to understand what motivates the other person, why they do what they do, and I don't offer solutions until the other person has *fully* explained themselves. All this is happening because I'm not glancing at my watch because I've said yes to too many obligations. I become an improved listener because I've said no to the trivial, the unimportant.

If you were to say yes to a request that, deep down inside, you don't want to do, what happens? Often the outcome is to become resentful and direct that resentment toward the person doing the asking. If the person is important in your life, the last thing you need percolating inside you is resentment. Instead, offer alternative plans. You are leaving the door open. If the person is not of great importance in your life, a simple no thank you is sufficient. By declining the request, you created time for yourself and perhaps for someone who *is* central in your life. That could be your partner, your children, or someone needing a helping hand. Again, nothing selfish about that!

| | |

TRY IT:

- Try to think back over the last month and list when you said yes and later wished you hadn't. This simple exercise primes you to respond differently to the next request or activity that you truly do not want to do.

- Strive to be a better listener by carving out more time for yourself to create a calmer, more patient you. Remind yourself that saying no is liberating, and everyone around you ultimately benefits. Saying no often allows for yeses to new experiences.

WRITE THE ONE TAKE-AWAY FROM THIS CHAPTER THAT WILL GIVE YOU THE MOST BENEFIT AND YOU WILL WORK ON DAILY.

_____

_____

_____

_____

_____

_____

_____

_____

_____

_____

_____

_____

_____

_____

_____

_____

_____

_____

_____

_____

_____

NO AND NEGOTIATIONS, OPERATING YOUR OWN BUSINESS, OR MANAGING A DEPARTMENT

If you are looking for a gem, you have to cast aside a lot of plain old rocks.

To successfully manage your own business or a large department within a business, every day is a test of your prioritization skills. Without that skill, you will find yourself pulled in a million different directions. It is essential to whittle your "to-do" list down to only the essential core activities that will best help you reach your goal.

Known as the 80/20 rule, this accurate adage espouses that 80 percent of the results come from only 20 percent of the activities. In general, I've found this to be true, and I'm always trying to glean which activities are driving the best results. As I uncover them, I go into a laser-like focus on those and ignore the activities that don't make the cut. I know when I'm on the right track when an offer or activity leads to a clear feeling; if it feels like an annoyance, I say no, but if I get a vibe of excitement, I say, "Absolutely, heck yes!"

When you are cognizant of the 80/20 rule, you notice that it has applications even beyond business. For example, you might find that you get 80 percent of your happiness from 20 percent of your friends and relatives. Billionaire Warren Buffet probably subscribes to an even stricter rule than 80/20, perhaps 90/10, because he said, "The difference between successful people and very successful people is that very successful people say no to almost everything."

The key to this concept is to let some activities go and just focus on the ones that have the best returns. In sales, that might mean zeroing in on your best customers and giving them top service while dropping those who are a pain in the ass and taking up a disproportionate use of your time. It might seem counterintuitive in a sales position to be saying "no" quite often, but by doing so, you will be giving your best customers the red carpet and probably generate even more business. This practice will allow you to go out and find more customers who fit a similar profile of yielding great results. Keep the 80/20 rule in mind, and it will help you create more time while assisting you in cutting the cord to a never-ending to-do list.

Running a business or a department entails frequently saying no. Your persona at your business should be tougher than in your personal life. Leave emotion at the door; it's business, and it's your time. I'm pitched ideas for writing and speaking quite often. When I became known as the author of several survival and rescue books, people would track me down and pitch me an idea of why their story would be perfect for me. I reject 99 percent of them because they don't meet my standard of sustaining an entire book in an edge-of-your-seat manner. And the 1 percent that I don't reject, I investigate, and probably half of those don't feel right. That means 99.5 percent of the time I'm saying no. It's not hard to do once you've done it a few times. If you are looking for a gem, you have to cast aside a lot of plain old rocks.

Another author I know, far more successful than me, shuts off every distraction possible when focused on a project. He says no to every high-paid speaking request that comes his way, every solicitation to help a fundraiser, every interview request. He will have time for those after the task is completed. He lives and breathes the project he is working on and doesn't want to be pulled from the momentum. Whatever endeavor you're working on, whatever goal you have set for your department—go after it with a single-minded focus and say no to the ancillary requests coming your way.

Yet another tact is to give a temporary no to business opportunities you don't have time for—after all, the day may come when you need them. If I'm asked to speak and have other priorities, I'll say, "I'm unable at this time, but I'll keep your information for when my schedule opens up." Or I might direct the requester to a speaker just starting out; that way, everyone wins. Sometimes a partial yes yields a positive outcome. I was recently asked to review and edit a manuscript and name my price. The timing was wrong, so I countered with, "I can devote ten hours to the task and give you a three-page summary of overall improvements I recommend, but I won't line edit." The writer was more than happy with this arrangement.

CUSTOMERS

When you first open your business, you want customers, and you will find yourself saying yes quite often, but once your business is established, you want to focus on retaining the best, key customers. How do you do that? By saying no to the things that pull you from your core mission so that you can concentrate on the product or service you are offering. When I feel overwhelmed, I pretend I'm the president of the United States. Imagine how easy it would be for them to be bombarded by every problem that the country is experiencing. Instead, an effective president has laid out their agenda and tackles what they view as the most important problems first. And how do they keep out all the other issues and people vying for a piece of their time? They have a chief of staff. In your business or department, you need to be your own chief of staff. When I managed a department at an insurance company, and later in my speaking and writing career, I put my chief of staff hat on at the end of the day and wrote down the top priorities for the next day. That simple act helped keep me focused and on track and avoid flitting from one issue to another as they popped up.

Once you have established a fair price—one that makes you a profit but is attractive to customers—there will be times when a prospective customer tries and talk you down. I've found it best to stick with the price you think is fair, or as Carol Tome, the CEO of UPS, said in a *Wall Street Journal* interview, "If a customer isn't willing to pay and they elect to leave us, then we wish them the best." The article was titled "This UPS CEO Preaches the Power of No" and explained how she shifted the focus to the bottom line and weeded out less-profitable customers. Her focus is to transition the company to be "better, not bigger." You may want to do the same.

In that same *Wall Street Journal* article, Tome showed flexibility in another area, the employees. In her first six months on the job, she talked with workers across all departments, "asking them what worked and what didn't." During those conversations, she learned that the company was having trouble retaining some of its African American employees because of rigid dress codes, "which banned beards or traditionally Black hairstyles like Afros or braids." Tome relaxed those rules to "celebrate diversity rather than corporate restrictions." That's a good lesson for all of us—say yes to listening to people who are on the front lines.

NEGOTIATIONS

In negotiations to buy a costly item for your business, or for that matter, your personal life, saying no and being prepared to walk away is the best way I know to arrive at the lowest price. The pressure, in most cases, is on the seller, not the buyer. The seller is usually anxious to complete the deal in a set time period; that's why sellers often say, "for a limited time only." As the buyer, you need to show discipline to resist the pressure, and by doing so, you are likely to get a better deal. I can't foresee any situation where you should spend a large sum of money when under pressure, or the spur of the moment, or based on emotion because you got swept up in the "once in a lifetime offer." In most cases, the item you want to buy will be there the next day, and often at a slightly lower price.

I've probably bought twenty new cars in my life, and I learned "our best offer" was usually nothing of the sort. In general, the more I said no, the more the price came down. It wasn't until the seller said no to *my offer* that they were near the bottom of what they could sell the car for and still make a small profit.

The process of finding the lowest price is like my description of knowing your value at your workplace. Sometimes the only sure way to find that value is to interview at other companies. The same goes with negotiations on a purchase; you get a sense of the lowest price by talking to different dealers: you are doing reconnaissance and gathering information along the way. The more the seller used high-pressure tactics, the more I distrusted them. (And one time, my suspicions were dead-on because when it came time to sign the paperwork, the price was different than was verbally quoted to me.)

TIME OFF

One of the biggest pitfalls for a small business owner is having the job consume you. You need to say no to working around the clock. Here's my example: I make time to get away from my work, which often means going to my remote cabin in the hills of northern Vermont. That has been my sanctuary for over forty years. Recently, I learned that technology had invaded that sacred space. My cell phone was able to display emails. Imagine how tempting it was to check them. But I made a rule: don't turn the damned thing on. Instead, I reminded myself that this was my retreat to unplug and think. I'm not here to do administrative work. Maybe I'll write while at the cabin, but my main activities are to swim, bike, hike, and cut firewood. I don't want the cell phone to interrupt my connection with nature and the inner silence from being alone.

Find your place to unplug from the electronic leash. Go there and recharge your mind—the emails and the challenges will be there when you get back. You own your business; don't let it own you.

Many successful people I know do not work longer hours than the population at large. By taking time for proper sleep and exercise, they know they can perform better. They are not workaholics but rather more efficient with their time than others. They are mindful of where their working hours are spent and the same with their personal time. And vacations are an important part of that mix. Energy and enthusiasm are what counts, not the number of hours poured into a job. Your enthusiasm is contagious, and customers will love it.

TRY IT:

- Write a core statement of your primary intention for your business or career. It will help you from being pushed, pulled, and pressured to put your energy elsewhere. When a request comes your way, ask yourself, "Will this help my core objective along? Will this matter in the long run?" If not, say no. Make an agenda, and stick to it.

- Always remind yourself that most projects take at least twice as long as you think. Knowing this helps you set a fair price for taking on a new endeavor, as well as walk away from those where you don't feel fairly compensated.

- In negotiations, don't get caught up in the moment. Unless you have done your homework and truly know the fair price, never be pressured that you must act now, or the "deal" will be gone. Instead, be cool, calm, and unemotional. Whoever is making the offer should always allow you the proper amount of time to think about it. In my experience, about eight times out of ten, if you say, "No, thank you," the deal gets sweeter.

- Apply the 80/20 rule to various aspects of your life, beyond business. While writing this chapter, I had to laugh because I'm guilty of ignoring the concept of my fishing hobby. I own a truckload of fishing lures. But only about 5 percent of those lures are the ones that are the most successful. Why am I even lugging around the others? Slowly I'm removing the non-performers from my tackle, and I'm perfecting the presentation of the ones that work the best. And perhaps best of all, I don't go chasing after every "latest and greatest" new lure on the market, saving hundreds of dollars in the process.

CONSIDER RUNNING YOUR OWN BUSINESS

Are you working for a company that is stressing you out?

Do you wish you had entered a different field?

Are you nearing retirement but need extra money?

If you answered yes to any of these questions, don't let anyone tell you that it's too late to make a change. I have a friend who went through all the trials and tribulations of law school, the bar exam, and working for a large law firm, only to realize being an attorney made him unhappy. Instead of feeling trapped, he thought about what he liked to do—build things—and he recalled an earlier job that he enjoyed as a representative for a national lumber company. He saved his money, and after a few years in law, bought a lumberyard. He's been happy ever since.

My escape from the insurance industry took longer than my attorney friend. I slowly transitioned out: first by moonlighting as a writer, then by finding a part-time job at an insurance company, and finally, after many years, became a full-time writer and speaker. You can do the same. By saving up a cushion of money and finding a part-time job with flexible hours, you can slowly build your new career or business. Some friends have even turned their hobbies into careers. Sure, it was a slow process that involved sacrifices and initially cutting back on spending, but imagine waking up in the morning and doing something that you enjoy and getting paid for it. If you decide to go this route, read all you can about how people made the change, and if possible, talk to people in the field you want to transition to.

**WRITE THE ONE TAKE-AWAY FROM THIS CHAPTER
THAT WILL GIVE YOU THE MOST BENEFIT AND YOU
WILL WORK ON DAILY.**

_____

_____

_____

_____

_____

_____

_____

_____

_____

_____

_____

_____

_____

_____

_____

_____

_____

_____

_____

_____

NO TO FEAR AND WORRY

In this chapter, we are not trying to abolish fear and worry, because we all experience them from time to time. Our focus is on handling those emotions when they come, minimizing them, and keeping them in the proper perspective. We are saying no to becoming *captive* to fear and worry. Our goal is to function despite fear and worry while mitigating their ramifications rather than eliminating them.

Most fear—except the primal fear that comes when you are physically threatened—is usually a built-in resistance to change and uncertainty. Rather than run from the emotion of fear, accept it and then find its root cause. Once you identify the underlying cause, start the process of putting the fear in its place. Ask yourself, "Will it matter in twenty years?" What is the worst that can happen? Chances are that the worst will never come, but even if it does, you will be able to handle it. You probably have forgotten that somewhere in your past, you went through an event just as harrowing and came out the other side.

One of the top fears people continually list when polled is public speaking. Here's a confession: I was once one of those people. Now you're probably saying, "Now, wait a minute;

hasn't this writer repeatedly mentioned his life as an author *and* as a professional speaker?" The answer is yes, and that's why I'm using this element of my fear to share, showing you how far I've come once I confronted my fear and set about to change it. I'm proud that I did not let it paralyze me and have it rule what I could or could not do. Instead, I channeled that fear into purposeful action to conquer it, and you can, too. When I was in college, I avoided classes where I knew oral presentations were required. I'd had a couple of bad experiences where my nerves got the best of me, and like most people, I did what I could to avoid the same thing again. Later, when I worked for a corporation, I realized I could no longer duck giving presentations, and I did one of the smartest things I could have done for myself and my career: I took an evening course in public speaking. In this classroom were people of all ages and different backgrounds, but we all had one thing in common: a deep-seated dread of speaking in front of groups.

How did we conquer our fear? By confronting it and practicing. We gave frequent presentations in the classroom, and the instructor and fellow students were encouraging as we stumbled through our mini speeches. The more talks I gave, the more comfortable I became. Years later, when my first book was published, I knew that I'd have to give talks to the public to promote it. I was far from a polished speaker, but I said yes to every opportunity, knowing the more talks

156

I gave, the more confident I'd become. After a year or two, I found myself looking forward to giving presentations, and developed a style all my own, never using a single note. Fast forward a few years later. Several speaking bureaus represented me, and I was hired to speak across the country and well paid for my time. *I went from fear of speaking to loving speaking so much that I made a career out of it.* If I can do it, anyone can. Fear was my motivator. Without that original fear, I might not have taken the speaking course, which led to me giving talks, which flowered into a speaking career, which led me to want to help others by teaching adult education courses on public speaking. I look back at all this and think about how remarkable the journey was because I took action despite my fear. Whatever your fear, there are therapists, courses, and your determination to practice overcoming it.

Many of the bravest people on the planet freely admit to feeling fear but manage not to let that fear paralyze them in the face of a dangerous job. When I was researching my cowritten book *The Finest Hours*, about the Coast Guard's greatest small-boat rescue, I spent many phone calls talking to the hero of the story, Bernie Webber. Bernie repeatedly told me he felt fear, trepidation, and dread about taking a thirty-six-foot wooden boat out into a blizzard producing forty-foot seas. He thought he was being sent on a "suicide mission." But he had signed up with the Coast Guard to save lives—and on this rescue, thirty-three sailors were on a sinking half of an oil tanker that faced imminent death—so Bernie knew he had to go. He kept his fear from overwhelming him by focusing on each task at hand during the rescue attempt and trying not to think about the long odds of pulling them all off successfully. Bernie did not let his fear make a coward out of him but rather became one of the Coast Guard's greatest heroes by performing his mission, despite the fear he never denied.

One last comment on fear. Never let it silence you into becoming a meek wallflower. Martin Luther King, Jr. wrote about this very trap when describing one of the most brutal and segregated cities back in his day. "Certainly, Birmingham had its decent white citizens who privately deplored the mistreatment of Negroes. But they remained publicly silent. It was a silence born of fear—fear of social, political, and economic reprisals. The ultimate tragedy of Birmingham was not the brutality of the bad people, but the silence of the good people."

NO WILL SET YOU FREE

WORRY

Worry is the sister to fear, where we stress over something that may or may not happen. And often, the thing we worry over is beyond our control, so the advanced worry does us no good. It is the ultimate waste of time.

Here's a more light-hearted look at worry, but it speaks volumes:

> "I have been through some terrible things in my life, some of which actually happened."
>
> —Mark Twain

Let's look at an example. You are driving like a madman because you are worried you will be late. Is it worth risking your life to be on time? No! So how do you calm yourself? It's easy: you are not late until you get there. In other words, the event you are worried about hasn't even happened, and it may not happen.

This book is all about taking back your time, and to me, the ultimate folly is giving your time or energy to the potential of something happening beyond your control. And suppose you cannot stop your mind from churning? Then research what you fear and worry about, see if there is anything you can do to mitigate the event if it happens, and then forget about it. (Or tell yourself, *I'll worry about it when it happens.*)

Another destructive by-product of worry, and why you should do your best to say no to it, is that worry chews up your now time. Your mind drifts off to a make-believe future of negativity, and in the process of worrying about a "maybe," you have missed out on present moments. When you find yourself in this "lifeboat" drifting to apprehension, take out the oars and change direction. You can do this by immersing yourself in an activity that keeps your mind occupied. Whether reading, exercising, gardening, calling a friend, or another distraction, do it to break the cycle of worry. I'm betting mankind is the only creature on the planet that worries—the other creatures are living in the moment and are *doing*. We can too.

TRY IT:

- When you find yourself worrying, have that internal self-talk that says *I'm wasting my time immobilizing myself over something that may or may not happen.* Then change the channel.

- If you are worried about another person, skip the worry part, and go straight to the source—reach out to the person and see what you can do to help their situation. Worrying is not helping them!

- Don't buy into the cultural brainwashing that because you care about someone, worrying is only natural. Instead, focus on the things you can control. Worrying will not change anything, so recognize when you fall into the void of thinking a bunch of bad things may happen and immediately replace it with the statement, "Whatever comes, I'll handle it the best I can." Then let it go.

RECOGNIZE WHEN FEAR IS HOLDING YOU BACK

Do you stay in a bad relationship because you're afraid of being alone?

Do you stay in a dead-end job because of the uncertainty of moving to a new job?

You avoid a new hobby, sport, or activity because you think your performance will be awful.

You avoid new destinations because of the unknown.

Certain topics are off-limits because they may cause discomfort of confrontation.

WRITE THE ONE TAKE-AWAY FROM THIS CHAPTER THAT WILL GIVE YOU THE MOST BENEFIT AND YOU WILL WORK ON DAILY.

_____

_____

_____

_____

_____

_____

_____

_____

_____

_____

_____

_____

_____

_____

_____

_____

_____

_____

NO AND YOUR MONEY

Chances are there is nothing you need right this minute. Assuming you have food, clothing, shelter, and a means of transportation (either your car or public transportation), the item that seems like a "must-have" is not.

I'm hoping most of you reading this don't need many of the tips and reinforcement outlined in this chapter, but the data about Americans and their finances indicates we have a long way to go.

NO TO DEBT

Buying a home versus renting depends on your unique financial situation and lifestyle tastes. But if you do decide to buy a home, your home mortgage is the only kind of debt that is beneficial; instead of paying a stranger rent, you are slowly building equity. All other debt is financial suicide. Credit card debt at exorbitant interest rates is a black hole difficult to climb out of. (The average household with credit card debt pays $1,300 in interest a year, according to Nerd-Wallet.) Of all the possible ways to get into debt, the credit card is usually the worst because of the interest rates. If you can't pay off your credit card balance in full at the end of each month, stop using it. The buy-now-and-pay-later approach is for suckers. If you can't afford to pay for an item in full, simply wait until you can.

If you are already up to your eyeballs in debt, take steps immediately to work with a nonprofit consumer credit counselor to methodically pay it down. Part of that solution will be paying off the debt with the highest interest rates charged first and the lowest last. Or it may involve a loan at a lower rate than your various debts, paying them all off with the loan, and then paying down the loan on a set basis.

NO TO "I'LL SAVE LATER"

Einstein reportedly said the most powerful force in the universe is "compound interest." I'm not sure I'd go that far, but the sooner you get your money working for you in whatever investment you choose, time is your ally. You begin to make money not only on your initial principal but on the gains you are earning.

A specific but realistic saving pattern is the way to go. For example, maybe you can save only 3 percent of your salary or income when starting your first job. As you get raises or your business grows, the 3 percent will be based on a larger amount, and more importantly, as your income grows, you can raise the 3 percent to 4 percent, then to 5 percent, and so on. Having your savings on autopilot where the amount is taken out of your paycheck or your checking account weekly is another key to getting started and keeping the savings flowing. If you work for a company with a 401K where the company matches a part of your contributions, you would be nuts not to take full advantage of it. And if you are self-employed, there are several different vehicles for savings, with my favorite being the Roth IRA, where your money grows tax-free. *No Will Set You Free* is not an investment book, but I urge anyone who doesn't grasp financial basics to go to the library and get a book for beginners.

When it comes to the stock market, research has shown that slow and steady wins the race. By that, I mean buying into the stock market with set periodic amounts (preferably through your 401K or into your Roth IRA). This is called dollar-cost averaging, meaning you are buying into the market at whatever its value is during your weekly purchases, ensuring that you are not dumping all your money in during a market high only to see the value plummet. I once tried to time the market by thinking I could gauge when it was low and a good time to buy. I also thought I'd recognize when it was at unwarranted highs and a good time to sell. It ended in disaster because I sold stocks far too early and missed several years of a bull market. Even experts who live, eat, and drink stock market data all day rarely get market timing right.

Just as small steps are essential to financial freedom, procrastination will keep you in chains. Some people will say they can't start saving now because their expenses are too high. But examine some of those expenses, and you might find some easy money by saying no to a few things that bring you little joy. Examples? Maybe you buy your lunch every day—try making your lunch and save six dollars per day. You might say eight bucks isn't much, but take that and multiply it times the number of days in a year you are at your job, then multiply that by ten years, and then factor in a rate of return of 5 percent yearly of investing that money and watch Einstein's statement take wing and soar. Other expenses you might cut are a high cable bill for TV extras you rarely watch, the ten pairs of shoes you bought and rarely wore, the health club membership you rarely use, the latest electronic gizmo, the expensive vacation where you might have had a more relaxing time staying home and making a day trip or two, and the list can go on once you set your mind to it. Say no to being trapped financially and yes to the wonderful sense of freedom resulting from financial independence.

HOME MORTGAGE

I mentioned the home mortgage was an acceptable form of debt, but that doesn't mean you shouldn't speed up the payments and own your house outright. When I bought my first house many years ago, I asked the bank to send me the amortization schedule for my loan. Boy, was that eye-opening. It showed how, during the first few years of the mortgage, most of my payments went to interest rather than principal, but in the later years, the opposite was true. And so, I'd send in a couple of extra payments of upcoming principal. That jumped me ahead in the schedule, meaning I skipped paying interest on the months I paid in advance. In essence, my extra principal payments reduced my mortgage term and saved me thousands of dollars in interest. You can accomplish something similar with a fifteen-year mortgage rather than a thirty-year one. The only drawback to the fifteen-year mortgage is that you are obligated to pay a higher monthly payment rather than when you have extra money.

Financial planners rarely advise paying off a mortgage because they are focused on the slight tax saving on interest paid or on a low interest rate compared to the return you would get investing that money in the stock market. That can be advantageous if the stock market goes up but backfire in a long bear market. But the main thing financial advisors often miss is the feeling of freedom of owning your home outright. No matter what happens with the economy or your job, *you own your home, not the bank,* and without monthly payments to meet, you can breeze through economic downturns. And unlike the stock market, paying down your mortgage via extra principal payments is a sure thing, and you will be able to see exactly how much in interest you save. Even if you are unsure what to do or simply do not have an extra dime to pay down your mortgage, insist the bank send you the amortization table for your loan and look at it often. It will give you the incentive in the future to want to pay a little extra in principal and avoid those big interest payments while moving you toward true homeownership faster. (Before you start making those extra payments, make sure you are contributing the full amount that your company will match on your 401K. I'm shocked when people tell me they don't do that, and my response is, "Would you turn down a raise? That is what you are doing if you don't contribute your portion.")

FINANCIAL PLANNERS

If you decide to work with a certified financial planner, it's best to choose one that is fee-only, preferably one that charges by the hour and can give you the amount of their fee after a couple of meetings with you. These types of planners have a legal fiduciary responsibility to work with your best interests in mind with no conflict of interest. If a financial planner claims there is no cost to you, red flags should go up. That means they work on commission, and you can be sure they will direct your money into an investment that pays them a handsome commission without keeping your best interests in line. Run from any advisor that's trying to sell you a specific product.

Target dated funds might be better than spending your money on a financial planner. These funds shift to more conservative investments as you get closer to your retirement, with the concept being that you should take less risk as you get older and have fewer years to recoup a loss.

NEGOTIATIONS

With negotiations, you need to be prepared to walk away, and it's best to have more than one suiter or buyer. An example is buying a car. Once you have selected the make and model, don't agree to what the first dealer says is their best price. Do some research online, travel to another dealer, and see what their best price is. When they ask you what you would pay, say a ridiculously low sum that you know they would never accept. Then go to a third dealer, and so on. Soon, you will know where the bottom price is. Sellers will pressure you by saying if you don't buy now, the offer is gone. I've found that is seldom the case. If the salesman can make a small commission and the dealer can profit, they will be more than happy to continue the negotiations.

Comparison shopping is the way to go, not just for cars, but for any large purchase.

NO TO "I NEED THIS NOW"

Chances are there is nothing you need right this minute. Assuming you have food, clothing, shelter, and a means of transportation (either your car or public transportation), the item that seems like a must-have is not. Wait until you can afford it. Or better yet, take the time to reconsider your need for the item. In this case, delaying a major purchase can work in your favor. Ask yourself, "Am I sure I'm going to use and enjoy this?" We have all bought things on impulse that now gather dust in the back of a closet, garage, or basement. There is a reason most Americans have clutter throughout their house—a good portion of it are items that were used for a short time and then lost their appeal.

One way to avoid impulse buying either while shopping in stores or online is to have a list of what you *really need*, and not get distracted by something not on the list. It will take discipline, but it will soon become a good habit. Of course, if you have loads of money, carry no debt, and your financial future is secured, treat yourself to items you think will bring you joy. The list for me is small. I feel blessed that I don't want any more possessions, and I'm reminded of Benjamin Franklin's saying, "He who multiplies riches, multiplies cares."

Helen and Scott Nearing, authors of *Living the Good Life*, had a similar view to Benjamin Franklin. They pointed out that the consumer system in America can enslave us, and the "only real freedom exists in minimizing needs."

More possessions will not bring you happiness. Say no to the impulse to buy now. Instead, wait a few days, and if that desire for the product is just as strong, go ahead and make the purchase—but only if you can pay in full.

NO TO ENDLESS GIFT-GIVING

Consider simplifying holidays and birthdays with their end-less commercialism by exchanging less expensive gifts or giving the gift of time. I've told my loved ones I don't need them to feel like they must buy me a gift, but instead, give me the gift of time. One person created a book of our trips over the last year told in pictures with captions; another illustrated an elaborate birthday card that had me laughing for five minutes; another said they were taking me fishing on their boat. These gifts from the heart were far better than me receiving an item I don't need, paid for with money my loved ones could use for their financial future.

TRY IT:

- I've just scratched the surface here on money, so be sure to find an easy-to-read book about personal finance. This topic should be required courses in high school and college because every person needs this knowledge, but unfortunately, personal finance is seldom taught.

- Say no to any offers you feel are high pressure and if the person pressuring is coming on strong. They are preying on your fear of missing out. The opportunity will be there after you have time to investigate.

- If you are told the deal will be gone if you don't accept now, walk away. In most cases, the deal will still be there, or you can make a transaction with another person down the road after you have had more time to think about the offer.

- Anyone offering big returns on your money—far bigger returns than your friends are making—should prompt a red flag. There is usually a catch in the fine print. If a "too good to be true" type of feeling hits you, it is probably a scam.

- As sure as day gives way to night, we will experience another recession, but wouldn't it be nice if you have done some preparation of saving and eliminating debt so you can ride it out without fear?

WRITE THE ONE TAKE-AWAY FROM THIS CHAPTER THAT WILL GIVE YOU THE MOST BENEFIT AND YOU WILL WORK ON DAILY.

_____

_____

_____

_____

_____

_____

_____

_____

_____

_____

_____

_____

_____

_____

_____

_____

WHEN YOU ARE THE REQUESTER

The answer is always no unless you ask.

This will be a short and sweet chapter because it's not about saying no but rather about getting someone else to say yes. People are reluctant to ask for a favor or assistance because they assume the answer will be no. Don't make that assumption because many people sincerely want to help you if the request is not too onerous.

This should be your motto: "The answer is always no unless you ask." There is rarely a downside to coming right out and asking what you want. The person can say yes, no, or maybe, so you have nothing to lose by asking.

Here's an example that I was involved in three months ago. A stranger ordered a book from me via my website, and I noticed she lived on a street on an ocean bay with which I was familiar. On a whim, I sent her an email, asking if she'd mind if I left my kayak on her section of the beach so I could use it over the next two weeks? It was summer, and there was good striped bass fishing in the bay. The woman said no problem. I brought my kayak down and left it behind her house. Over the next three months, every time I used the kayak, the woman happened to be home, and we became friends. Each time I drove down to kayak, I brought her a simple gift: one of my books, cucumbers and tomatoes from my garden, and even a fresh filet of a fish I caught while in my kayak. From that one simple "ask" of mine, I made a new friend, enjoyed fishing, swimming, and kayaking, and the woman received the gift of friendship and satisfaction, knowing she made someone happy with her yes. (And her yes involved no time on her part and no inconvenience.)

Reflecting on the kayak example, had I thought of it, I could have initially sweetened the request by saying, "I'll bring you fresh vegetables and the occasional filet in exchange for using your beach." Some requests lend themselves to offering a thank-you gift. Others don't; you just have to lay out what you are trying to accomplish and how others can help. Again, most people are kind at heart, and you will be surprised how many people are willing to help if little time on their part is required.

When you are the requestor, it's essential to be polite, clearly explain what you are asking for, and if it involves a time commitment from the other person, try to give an accurate estimate. We have learned that when we say no, it is not selfish or disrespectful, so you shouldn't take it that way if another person says no to your request. But don't ever hold back from asking what you want. You don't want to look back on your life and have regrets because you didn't try. The regret could be something big: *What would my life have been like if I had asked that person I liked on a date? What would my career have been like if I made a more forceful case to be promoted?* Or the regret might be small, but still a regret, nevertheless. Remember, when asked to analyze regrets in their life, most people cite not trying something or taking advantage of an opportunity rather than having regrets over making a bad decision or doing something that didn't work out. When we try and don't succeed, we quickly move on, but there is a long-lasting sting when we think "what might have been" because we didn't act.

One last example with a bit of humor. Just four days before writing this chapter, I went to a bank to get a document notarized. While in the notary's office, he said I needed two witnesses, and he wasn't allowed to ask other bank employees to witness the signing. I looked out at the lobby and said, "What about the customers out there?" He answered, "Don't even bother; the customers are always in a hurry." He was implying that I shouldn't ask them but did not specifically say I couldn't. So I stepped out of his office onto the lobby floor and said in a loud voice, "Excuse me, can two of you customers witness me signing a document? It will only take a minute." Two of the three customers turned to look at

NO WILL SET YOU FREE

me, hesitated, then said, "Sure, just as soon as we make our deposits."

I turned back to the notary, and he said, "Well, I didn't expect that." I'm not sure if he was referring to the bold way I asked customers the request or that they readily accepted. But no matter, the customers entered the office, witnessed the signing, and then signed their names. I thanked them profusely. One said, "No problem," and the other said, "It was my pleasure."

Say no to being timid about requesting favors, and remember the answer is always no unless you ask.

I I I

TRY IT:

- The next time you need a hand, overcome your shyness and reluctance to ask for help and instead, approach a few people until you get that yes.

- To increase your comfort level with strangers, next time you are in a store or waiting in a line, strike up a conversation, or better yet, ask a question. I'm betting 99 percent of the time that the stranger will engage politely.

- If your request is directed at an individual and you get a no, try being persistent in a creative way to get your yes. When I was researching my *New York Times* bestseller, *The Finest Hours*, the hero of the story, Bernie Webber, originally turned me down when I called him and asked if I could interview him. This would be a lengthy giving of his time, and he decided he didn't want to commit the time to recount his rescue story for a total stranger. But I didn't give up. I sent him one of my earlier rescue books, then waited a month and called him back. I asked if he enjoyed the book I sent, and he said yes. I asked if he would work with me on his story, and he said no. So what did I do? I sent him another rescue book I'd written, then a month later called again. This time, when I asked him to work with me, he said, "Let's do it on a trial basis." As we got to know one another, that trial basis turned into a permanent collaboration and friendship. His daughter later confided in me that Bernie called her and said something to the effect of, "Author Michael Tougias is persistent, but I can tell he is enthusiastic and committed, so I said yes to working with him."

WRITE THE ONE TAKE-AWAY FROM THIS CHAPTER THAT WILL GIVE YOU THE MOST BENEFIT AND YOU WILL WORK ON DAILY.

_____

_____

_____

_____

_____

_____

_____

_____

_____

_____

_____

_____

_____

_____

_____

_____

_____

HISTORIC NO'S AND NO'S OF CONVICTION AND CONSEQUENCE

We have talked about how the power of no can change our individual lives, but I also want to include some inspiring no's that were either historic or carried a heavy price in terms of the consequences that resulted from having strong conviction. These historic no's can motivate us to stand firm when we refuse to let injustice rule the day.

Most people are familiar with Martin Luther King Jr.'s March on Washington and the Selma to Montgomery March, but there is another earlier struggle where King flatly says no to injustice, no to delay, and no to rampant discrimination. This occurred while King was in solitary confinement after being arrested for his involvement in an equal rights, non-violent march in Birmingham without a permit. While he was confined, white ministers wrote an open letter to King that ran in the newspapers, calling for an end to the demonstrations. King decided to write back. I view his letter as an eloquently written "no manifesto" where he cannot abide by the status quo and will not postpone the demonstrations. His determination to buck the pressure of the white ministers is truly moving. Here are a few lines from his long response to the minister's request to cease and desist:

"I could not sit idly by in Atlanta and not be
concerned about what happens in Birmingham.
Injustice anywhere is a threat to justice everywhere.
You deplore the demonstrations taking place in
Birmingham. But your statement, I am sorry to say,
fails to express a similar concern for the conditions
that brought about the demonstrations...Birmingham
is probably the most thoroughly segregated city
in the United States. Its ugly record of brutality is
widely known. Negroes have experienced grossly
unjust treatment in the courts. There have been more
unsolved bombing of Negro homes and churches in
Birmingham than in any other city in the nation."

Later in the letter, King addresses the minister's call to postpone demonstrations until a more opportune time. King
flatly says no:

"We know through painful experience that freedom
is never voluntarily given by the oppressor; it must
be demanded by the oppressed. Frankly, I have yet
to engage in a direct-action campaign that was 'well
timed' in the view of those who have not suffered
unduly from the disease of segregation. Perhaps it is
easy for those who have never felt the stinging darts
of segregation to say 'Wait.' But when vicious mobs
lynch your mothers and fathers at will and drown
your sisters and brothers at whim; when you have
seen hate-filled policemen curse, kick and even kill

your black brothers and sisters; when you see the vast majority of your twenty million Negro brothers smother in an airtight cage of poverty in the midst of an affluent society; when you suddenly find your tongue twisted and your speech stammering as you seek to explain to your six-year-old daughter why she can't go to the public amusement park that has just been advertised on television and see tears welling up in her eyes when she is told that Funtown is closed to colored children, and see ominous clouds of inferiority begging to form in her little mental sky, and see her beginning to distort her personality by developing an unconscious bitterness toward white people…There comes a time when the cup of endurance runs over, and men are no longer willing to be plunged into the abyss of despair. I hope, sirs, you can understand our legitimate and unavoidable impatience."

Talk about a forceful, unapologetic no backed up with reasons! I urge readers to explore the letter Dr. King wrote in full. It is the ultimate no to injustice and yes to freedom.

III

Dr. King wrote the letter discussed in 1963, but earlier, in 1955, Rosa Parks decided she had had enough of segregation and humiliation and said no in a calm and dignified manner when told that she must give up her seat on a Montgomery

NO WILL SET YOU FREE

bus to a white male passenger who had just boarded. Parks declined to move. The bus driver insisted, but Rosa Parks held her ground even though she knew she would be arrested. Her decision was unplanned, but she could no longer go along with the injustice inflicted on her and other Black people. There was no need for her to explain her decision or to shout it out; she simply refused to move and stand in the back of the bus. Dr. King later described her "no" as one born out of "a sense of dignity and self-respect." Parks described her motive this way:

> "Our mistreatment was just not
> right, and I was tired of it."

Rosa Parks's refusal to move galvanized the Black community in Montgomery, where the incident occurred. Dr. King, E.D. Nixon, Rev. Ralph Abernathy, and other leaders were inspired by Parks, and they organized a bus boycott to draw attention to the treatment of Black people. Dr. King called the boycott "an act of massive noncooperation." Parks and King knew their actions were right, but sadly the racists of that period bombed King's house two months later. Parks and her husband were fired from their jobs and received death threats, causing them to move away from Montgomery. But Rosa Parks's courage to say no and live with the consequences brought worldwide attention to the scourge of segregation and mistreatment of Black people.

I I I

In October of 1962, at the height of the Cold War, a U-2 spy plane surveying Cuba discovered that Soviet forces had secretly installed nuclear missiles on the island. President John F. Kennedy immediately assembled a team of advisors from various government agencies, including the military. The group, "ExComm" (short for Executive Committee of the National Security Council), came to a consensus at their first emergency meeting that the Soviet missiles had to be taken out by military force. JFK said, "We're certainly going to do [option] one [an air strike]. We're going to take out those missiles." Others wanted stronger action: bombing all Cuban and Russian military sites in Cuba followed by an invasion. Even Bobby Kennedy thought a military strike was the only way to go: "Better to get it over with [war] and take our losses."

But over the next couple of days, as the spy planes gathered more intelligence, the president began to see that a military strike had the distinct possibility of starting WWIII and nuclear Armageddon. He began to consider other responses. Most of his advisors, and all the heads of the military branches, put pressure on the president to be forceful and stick with the military solution. JFK, however, said no to a military strike as the first option and instead proposed a blockade of Soviet ships heading for Cuba.

A couple of exchanges during the ExComm meeting between the president and his advisors illustrate this tension. General Curtis Lemay (head of the Air Force and Strategic Air Command) challenged Kennedy's resolve by saying there was no other solution than a massive military strike. Lemay even insulted the president, saying this about the blockade: "This is almost as bad as the appeasement at Munich." LeMay was referring to Neville Chamberlain's appeasement of Adolf Hitler.

Thankfully, Kennedy did not wilt under pressure, and instead of a surprise, full-scale military attack, which the Soviets surely would have responded to in kind, JFK used a combination of the blockade and diplomatic negotiations to keep the world from sliding into nuclear war.

JFK was not the only individual who said no during the Cuban Missile Crisis. Surprisingly, one of the key individuals who prevented a likely nuclear exchange was a Russian submarine commander Second Captain Vasily Arkhipov. He was on Soviet submarine B-59 commanded by Captain Savitsky. The sub was cruising the waters near the Blockade Line. A crew of seventy-eight men was on board, but only a few knew that the sub carried a nuclear-tipped torpedo, called a "special weapon."

United States Navy destroyers and the anti-submarine aircraft carrier *Randolph* detected the sub below them. The Pentagon had previously told the Soviets that if we located a sub, we would drop practice depth charges to announce that we had detected the sub, and it must surface immediately and then move away from the quarantine line. This information did not reach all the Soviet sub commanders because an exhausted Captain Savitsky became more and more unnerved as the depth charges exploded. He had no idea they were practice or dummy depth charges, and crewmen on the sub later recalled they sounded "like a sledgehammer on a metal barrel." Savitsky did not want to surface for fear of being captured or having his sub destroyed, and he stayed submerged despite low battery power and a build-up of dioxide inside the sub. The drama continued for four hours, with submariners feeling as if they were entombed inside a "metal barrel" tormented by pursuing ships.

Finally, a furious Captain Savitsky shouted, "Maybe the war has already started up there while we are doing summersaults here. We are going to blast them now! We will die, but we are going to sink them all." He then ordered the preparation to begin to have the nuclear torpedo fired. And he would have likely done that if not for the presence of Vasily Arkhipov, who argued they were not sure that war had broken out, nor had Moscow given them clearance to fire the nuclear torpedo. Arkhipov was successful, convincing the captain that the more prudent step would be to surface. Later, when Defense Secretary Robert McNamara learned of the details, he said, "We came very close [to nuclear war], closer than we knew at the time." Thomas Blanton, former director of the nongovernmental National Security Archive, went a step further: "A guy called Vasily Arkhipov saved the world."

III

One courageous no that changed world history for the better was Winston Churchill's refusal of Hitler's July 1940 offer of a truce. Hitler had already conquered many of the countries in Europe, and he had severely wounded the United Kingdom. Yet, he knew an invasion of England would be costly, and he was already setting his sights on invading Russia. By neutralizing England, Hitler could consolidate his power and focus his resources on attacking Russia. It's likely that after that, he would expand into even more countries, perhaps finishing off the UK or, at the least, control all of Europe under German power for decades. The US was not yet in the war, and only Britain stood between Hitler and the potential complete domination of Europe, Russia, and North Africa.

Here is what the United Press reported from Germany on July 19, 1940, regarding the peace proposal:

> "Hitler made it clear that rejection of his appeal to 'reason' would result in a final attack upon Britain. As he spoke, German airplanes ranged over the British Isles and dive-bombed British shipping in what the Nazi said was a mere preliminary offense...to invade England."

Churchill flatly refused the offer. Imagine what might have happened had Churchill taken the easy way out and tried to save Britain at the expense of Hitler controlling Europe? If Churchill had submitted, who knows where Hitler's reign of terror would have stopped.

There are countless other historical figures—from John Muir to Harriet Beecher Stowe—who said no to the status quo and helped make a difference. When I'm faced with pressure to conform or take a stand that seems difficult, I think of the people like Churchill, MLK, and JFK, and it inspires me to speak up.

WRITE THE ONE TAKE-AWAY FROM THIS CHAPTER THAT WILL GIVE YOU THE MOST BENEFIT AND YOU WILL WORK ON DAILY.

_____

_____

_____

_____

_____

_____

_____

_____

_____

_____

_____

_____

_____

_____

_____

_____

_____

_____

_____

_____

_____

SOME SHORT NO'S

NO TO PROLONGED HEARTACHE

Nobody leads a charmed life, and every one of us will have heartache from a crushing event. The stages of grief and depression are well documented and so are treatments. But I want to offer tips I've learned that *shorten* the heartache:

- The most important thing to remember is to *let time pass*. Know that as time passes, you will begin to feel better. While you may not feel a little stronger each day that passes, but instead may have ups and downs, overall, as the weeks go by, you will feel more resilient and less fragile.

- Go through the motions of living and being engaged with friends and family. You probably won't feel like doing anything but will force yourself to get out of your house or apartment. Fake it till you make it. Pretend you are floating through the days, simply doing your best to let time pass.

- Do cardio exercise. The endorphins released are just what you need.

- Make sure you have a support group. Reach out to friends and even acquaintances. Don't assume they understand how tough things are for you.

- Focus on the good things in your life, and when the gloom seems to dominate your thoughts, change the channel with the self-talk we outlined in the "No to Negativity" chapter.

- And finally, if you feel the depression and heartache are showing no signs of easing after several weeks, be sure to contact a therapist and consider an antidepressant to get you through the rough patch.

NO TO THE PITFALLS THAT CAN COME WITH SUCCESS

Why do so many incredibly successful people fall into alcohol, drugs, and excess in general? It's because they get on the hamster wheel of endless obligations, love the buzz from the success or the fame, and never slow down.

When you become successful, be sure it's a peaceful kind of success. You will get bombarded by invitations, advice, and interruptions. It's up to you to remember how you became successful in the first place: chances are, it was because you were super focused on the one or two things that you wanted to develop. You knew that to achieve your success, you would have to give some things up to zero in on the work it takes to reach your goal. Don't let success pull you in a million directions. Say no to everything that is not near and dear to your heart; avoid the hamster wheel at all costs.

Here is a quote from actress Renée Zellweger that shows us how to take back our time. "I got caught up in the cycle of obligations and pressures—the next project, the next product. It was time to learn something about myself, to do things for the sake of doing them." In *AARP* magazine, Zellweger went on to explain her unique view on aging and taking control: "I don't call it aging, I call it winning. It's just so much fun to say no and to do things you've wanted to try. You don't have to be perfect at something: just start walking toward it and see where the adventure goes."

Here's another example from Steve Jobs. In the book *The One Thing*, the author explains how when Jobs returned to Apple, "He was famously as proud of the products he didn't pursue as he was of the transformative products Apple created." He streamlined and cut the products offered or in development from 350 to 10. "Focusing," said Jobs, "is about saying no."

NO WILL SET YOU FREE

NO TO PETTY PEOPLE

People who make mountains out of molehills are among the ultimate time-wasters and you should have a strict no policy toward them. And by that, I mean don't take the bait to be drawn into their drama and instead ignore them.

Petty people are masters at going out of their way to make things more difficult than they are, and they want company in their self-induced misery. If you truly want to be liberated and have the time to focus on what's important to you, cut these petty people from your life. And you know the types I'm talking about: they create red tape where there is none, they have a ready list of grievances, they turn what should be a five-minute meeting into an hour. It's hard to fathom what drives petty people, but you can easily spot them by their complaining. Often, they have a little bit of authority which has gone to their head, and they rule their sphere of influence like a dictator of a banana republic. They never choose their battles wisely because they thrive on battles and create new ones to fill the void, aching for attention.

I once worked for a boss who was so petty, he pointed to an apple on my desk and told me that having it there didn't look professional. I couldn't help but smile, thinking of all the emergencies we were devoting our time to, yet his focus was on appearance. It was all I could do to stop myself from saying his thirty-year-old tie wasn't up to snuff! Nor did I point out that his sneaking out of the building for a cigarette was anything but professional, and that my apple was far healthier. Instead, I put the apple in my briefcase because, at the time, I was working on an important project, and the last thing I wanted was to be drawn into a debate over something so petty as an apple on my desk.

I've learned that petty people manufacture stress, enjoy arguing on almost any subject, and want company in their petty world. Elect to not enter their negative energy field but stay in your low-stress mindset, where you rarely do battle and don't let the little stuff bother you. The petty person wants to engage you in debate and take your focus off what's important. Just say no by taking the wind out of their sails with a quick resolution of the issue or, when possible, ignore them altogether.

I'll bet you can think of one or two people who fit this profile of pettiness, and if you see any of those signs in your own life, let the little stuff go. *No Will Set You Free* only works if you say no to those requests and people that chew up your precious time *and* you recognize when you are guilty of giving your energy to something relatively minor. Focus on what is truly relevant to your core values and goals and catch yourself when you begin to make a big deal out of something that shouldn't get more than a quick look in your rear-view mirror.

NO TO VICTIMHOOD

Remember that no matter how bad the situation, you always have one thing in your control: your reaction. Say no to the reaction of "I'm screwed," "Why me," or "What's wrong with me," which are all in the realm of victim mentality. That pessimistic mood over the long term not only slows you from bouncing back but it has been linked to cognitive decline in people over age fifty-five. Instead, you want to acknowledge the problem, know that it has likely happened to others, and reset your reaction to, "What can I learn from this?" "How can I gain something positive from this setback?" and "Good things are coming." Now, instead of being the victim, you are already bouncing back, hyper-aware of new opportunities that might present themselves. You are on the lookout for the positive.

It's also important to remind yourself of the good things you already have in your life—even the smallest of pleasures. You may find keeping a daily gratitude journal helps to keep you thinking, *I am strong and resilient* rather than, *I'll never recover*. You transition from victimhood to conqueror of your problem. Yes, it takes time, but your outlook is priming the pump for your next adventure, next love, and the next phase of your life, which very well may be the best period yet.

The key is how you interpret the event that has knocked you down. Are you a victim, or will you be the victor who overcomes all the challenges thrown at you? Psychotherapist and author Kim Schneiderman shows the two approaches using Dorothy from the *Wizard of Oz*. The victim approach would focus on the negative events that befell Dorothy: her dog was taken away, then she got hit by a tornado, and, to make matters worse, she then has to deal with a powerful witch out for revenge. Schneiderman points out a different interpretation, saying we should view Dorothy as "a brave girl [who] overcame obstacles, learned the importance of relationships, realized her own strength, and appreciated the value of home." I'd want to be that second Dorothy rather than the first, wouldn't you?

And you don't need to go it alone. Alcoholics Anonymous shows us that connecting with others who have been through the battle or are in the midst of the battle is extremely helpful. It relieves the isolation, and people share ideas of what works. And equally important, you become more compassionate to people struggling through whatever problem they are trying to overcome. There is a group for almost every challenge, and if not, employ the help of a good therapist. There is no shame in getting help. It's a temporary source of support, and often, the main benefit of working with others is the reinforcement you get that you are already on the right path.

To emerge from victimhood and become a conqueror of your ordeal, don't waste your precious energy blaming others. Let it go. Nurture yourself, reward yourself, and envision an even better life. It takes time and repetition, but this approach, reaction, and interpretation of a problem has worked for me, and it can work for you.

NO TO STICKING YOUR HEAD IN THE SAND

Too many of us let life happen to us rather than shape it. To shape it, make conscious decisions rather than decisions by default. If you do nothing, that is still a decision to remain with the status quo. We ignore some obvious signs that change is needed rather than confronting the issue, which can be uncomfortable. But I'd rather have some short-term pain in exchange for some long-term gain, so address the situation head-on rather than ignoring it, hoping it will go away.

NO TO MORE, MORE, MORE

Earlier I mentioned that almost every request you agree to takes much longer than expected. One way to more accurately predict how long something will take was explained in a study by Roger Buehler at Wilfrid Laurier University. When students were asked how long it would take to complete a term paper, almost all of them were overly optimistic, citing a time factor far lower than proved to be the case. But when other students were asked a similar question but encouraged to think how long similar projects took in the past, their estimate of time involved was for a longer period and much closer to reality. Another way to have a more accurate estimate is to break down all the steps you think will be involved before guessing at the time factor.

I mention our tendency to underestimate the time devoted to projects to keep us from giving a quick yes. It's not healthy to be a constant volunteer, helper, and assistant. We need to pick our spots, so we still have time to relax. Say no to the requests for more, more, more. You can only give so much.

The concept of more also applies to material possessions and the complexity we take on in our day-to-day lives. You might find yourself weighing the benefits of a high-paying job with never-ending hours. Yes, you will be able to buy whatever you want, except time. Some people have traded the big paycheck for a job with more fixed hours and learned to live with less. You might be one of those people who doesn't mind trading off consuming more in exchange for a simpler life where freedom is your most precious commodity. When I was fifty-two, I traded a job with sizable income and the trappings that went with it for a career with less income but the flexibility to spend a couple of hours each day out in nature, enjoying the sunlight. My last corporate job had me going to work in the dark and returning home in the dark, and I asked myself, *Is it worth it?* My answer was no, and I've never regretted the decision.

Henry David Thoreau said, "Many a forenoon have I stolen away, preferring to spend thus the most valued part of the day; for I was rich, if not in money, in sunny hours and summer days, and spent them lavishly." Thoreau was the master of living simply and saying no to the chains that bind us to the ever-increasing need for material possessions. You may not want to be as extreme as Thoreau but take the time to look inward and find the right balance.

INTUITION

Always listen to your intuition, and if that gut feeling says something's not right, start leaning in the direction of no to whatever the activity is you are considering. I've interviewed and studied over a hundred survivors who escaped from life-threatening accidents and situations and found many of them had a gut feeling that warned them something bad was coming. They ignored the feeling at their peril.

So what is intuition? My definition is that intuition is comprised of subconscious clues that you cannot yet articulate but are aware of the *feelings* they generate. (Usually, later, the clues become clear.) When I have to make a big decision, I might make a list of pros and cons, but if my intuition is strong, saying "go for it" or "don't do it," I'll listen and follow that gut feeling over the list. Sigmund Freud had an interesting view on this subject: "When making a decision of minor importance, I have always found it advantageous to consider all the pros and cons. In vital matters, however, the decision should come from the unconscious, from somewhere within."

If you are unsure what to do, try to stall for time. But don't ruminate about the decision; try to forget about it. Instead, disengage from churning about the issue by keeping your mind busy with something unrelated to your decision. This allows your unconscious mind to go to work. Soon enough, you will have that feel or vibe of which way to go. This happens because you slowed down and didn't force the decision. Instead, you took time off from trying to decide and let those clues percolate inside you until you *know* what to do. And if that doesn't work, pretend to choose a decision without telling anyone, then let time pass and see how you feel. Are you pumped, or do you have a nagging feeling something is not right? You now have your answer. Listen to those hunches!

The key to trusting your intuition is to slow down and not force it. That inner voice will usually lead you in the right direction, but only if you quiet yourself enough to be aware of it.

WRITE THE ONE TAKE-AWAY FROM THIS CHAPTER THAT WILL GIVE YOU THE MOST BENEFIT AND YOU WILL WORK ON DAILY.

_____

_____

_____

_____

_____

_____

_____

_____

_____

_____

_____

_____

_____

_____

_____

_____

_____

_____

_____

_____

FINAL THOUGHTS

Our journey is almost over, and I want to thank you for joining me. You now have the tools to take back your time, reduce stress in your life, and find your path to freedom. Freedom to focus on the people, activities, and work that are most important to you. Will it be easy? Let me answer that by saying that if you implement the techniques in this book with determination, the process will get easier as time passes, and with enough practice, mindful use of your time will become second nature.

Sure, there will be bumps in the road, but you only fail when you stop trying. If you have had a life-long habit of saying yes to everybody, the transition to polite no's will have setbacks. That is to be expected. Be aware of how you feel when you get the hang of reclaiming your time. It should spawn a sense of liberation and relaxation as you discover more time in the day for what brings you joy. Those positive feelings give you the reinforcement to continue to set boundaries with fewer distractions and demands on your time.

In the beginning of the book, I wrote: *"Once I learned that No could set me free, my life took off in various new directions—all of them more fulfilling than where I had been.*

We only have one life, and the most important aspect in our control is time: how, where, and with whom we portion it out. The trick is to use it the way you really want to and not get swept up by spending it the way others would have you handle it." Try to follow the message in those words daily. And if you need a little help from time to time, repeat these affirmations to help keep you on track:

- I will not feel guilty when I say no.

- I will not be pressured to do something that doesn't feel right.

- I'll listen closely to my intuition.

- "I'll get back to you," will be the phrase I use if I'm undecided.

- My key decision-making factor will be the question, "Will this bring me joy?"

- I will put the people I love first, and that might mean saying no to others.

- When I help others, it's not out of guilt or manipulation, but it is driven by love and knowing I can make a difference.

- I understand that at my place of employment, I now have techniques to use to push back on being overwhelmed with work without using the word no.

- I will not be pulled in a million directions but instead will live a life of intentions.

- I will put my health first. My body is the vehicle that takes me where I need to go.

- I will strive to have no regrets when my time on this planet is finished. Instead, I'll have a sense of peace that I didn't hold back and that I did my best to fulfill my dreams.

- I may not always have total control of each situation, but I have total control of my reaction and response.

- Successful people say no to almost everything beyond their core goals, and I am successful.

- I carve out time for my "passion project" so that I can give it my best shot.

- I now have the tools to say no to all the things holding me back: fear, worry, procrastination, perfectionism, and other negative emotions that keep me from realizing my potential.

- I am adaptable. I am resilient. I am lucky.

| | |

We now have the tools to say no more often, but each of us has a different area where they need to be applied. For example, I need to be more selective in choosing which writing and speaking ideas and opportunities to pursue. And to do that, I will need to say no more often. For someone else, it might be family obligations/requests or too much volunteering at work.

Think carefully about the areas where you are over-committing or intuitively know it's important to take back your time. Try to identify the top three or four areas where you want to make a change and what you need to do to fix the situation. Write each objective on a separate index card. Now give yourself a deadline to take the first step to address that area and put that target date at the top of the index card. I have found this simple act of identifying a specific goal and writing it down with a deadline to be helpful in achieving the desired outcome. Keep the index cards in a place you'll see them every day, and they will prompt you to act. Maybe one of your index cards will say, "I will have a conversation with my boss about focusing on fewer projects because I feel overwhelmed." Perhaps another will say, "I will have a talk with my friend about volunteering too much because I need some time for myself." Having a date at the top to start the ball rolling to address these areas will help keep you from procrastination. Remember, you are tackling these tough issues so that your health and well-being come first, and as a result, you will have more time and energy for what is truly important in your life. You and everyone around you will benefit.

A friend once told me, "It's where you set your gaze." She meant that if you are deliberate in how you want to conduct your life and where you want it to go, that's exactly what will happen. But if your gaze is set to petty, negative, or modest ambitions, that is where you will end up. On the other hand, if your gaze is fixed upon beauty, boldness, kindness, and meaningful impact, there's a good chance your path will be enjoyable and lead to fulfillment.

I wish you a life of balance involving the right mix of play, purposeful work, family time, and healthy living. One little word will help set you free; use it often and wisely.

ABOUT THE AUTHOR

Michael J. Tougias (pronounced *Toh-Gis*, hard G) is a lecturer and *New York Times* bestselling author and coauthor of thirty-one books for adults and eight for young adults and children.

Fatal Forecast: An Incredible True Tale of Disaster and Survival at Sea was praised by the *Los Angeles Times* as "a breathtaking book—Tougias spins a marvelous and terrifying story." *The Finest Hours,* which Tougias co-authored, tells the true story of the Coast Guard's most daring rescue. A finalist for the Massachusetts Book Award, the book was made into a movie by Disney. *Ten Hours Until Dawn: The True Story of Heroism and Tragedy Aboard the Can Do in the Blizzard of '78,* was selected by the American Library Association as one of the "Top Books of the Year" and described as a "white-knuckle read, the best book of its kind." His latest books are *A Storm Too Soon, Above & Beyond,* and a prequel to *There's a Porcupine in My Outhouse* titled *The Waters Between Us: A Boy, A Father, Outdoor Misadventures, and the Healing Power of Nature.*

Several of Tougias's books were adapted for middle readers (ages eight to thirteen) and chapter books with Macmillan.

His series is "The True Rescue Series," and it includes *Into the Blizzard, Attacked At Sea, A Storm Too Soon,* and *The Finest Hours.*

Michael Tougias has been featured on ABC's *20/20*, the Weather Channel, and NPR, among other appearances. He offers slide lectures for each of his books and speaks at libraries, lecture series, schools, and colleges across the country. He also speaks to business groups and associations on leadership and decision-making, including such programs as Leadership Lessons from the Finest Hours; Survival Lessons: Decision Making Under Pressure; and Fourteen Steps to Strategic Decision Making: JFK and the Cuban Missile Crisis. He lives in Florida and Massachusetts. For more information, videos of some of the rescues Tougias writes about, or to contact the author, visit www.michaeltougias.com.

Mango Publishing, established in 2014, publishes an eclectic list of books by diverse authors—both new and established voices—on topics ranging from business, personal growth, women's empowerment, LGBTQ studies, health, and spirituality to history, popular culture, time management, decluttering, lifestyle, mental wellness, aging, and sustainable living. We were recently named 2019 *and* 2020's #1 fastest-growing independent publisher by *Publishers Weekly*. Our success is driven by our main goal, which is to publish high-quality books that will entertain readers as well as make a positive difference in their lives.

Our readers are our most important resource; we value your input, suggestions, and ideas. We'd love to hear from you—after all, we are publishing books for you!

Please stay in touch with us and follow us at:
Facebook: Mango Publishing
Twitter: @MangoPublishing
Instagram: @MangoPublishing
LinkedIn: Mango Publishing
Pinterest: Mango Publishing
Newsletter: mangopublishinggroup.com/newsletter

Join us on Mango's journey to reinvent publishing, one book at a time.

Printed in the USA
CPSIA information can be obtained
at www.ICGtesting.com
JSHW031707290824
69005JS00003B/3